RED CROSS
ROLL CALL
JOIN
POST CARD

...onder Football Contest
Radio. Station
W.C.B.M.

baltimore. During the day many trips are enjoyed and from May to October, daily "Moonlight Rides"
down the bay are crowded with happy merry-makers.

TIMORE
AUG 25
8-PM
1950?

POST CARD

Dear Mr Parker
My Name Miss Dolores
Marx
Address- 2817 Berwick
Balto 14 Md
Phone Hamilton
TV WAAM 7490
Channel 13

Stop The Music Tele
Box 330
New York 19
New York

POST CARD

PRUNES 10¢
OAT MEAL WHEN YOU
CAN GET IT 20¢
VIRGINIA HAM
NICE+ TENDER 60¢
CHICKEN IN THE
ROUGH AS YOU
WANT IT #1.50

POST CARD
BUY U.S.S.
BOND
ASK YOUR POS...
THIS SIDE

ORE
JUN 23
6·30 PM
1931

Margere W. Smith
Conn State Coll,

THIS SPACE FOR WRITING MESSAGES. $4-

Heard the glad news
from John and
sincerely ...

BALTIMORE
NOV 25
9-PM
1916

POST

THIS SPACE FOR ADDRESS ONLY.

POST CARD

MESSAGE MAY BE WRITTEN ON

BALTIMORE, MD.
AUG 15
3-PM
1922

In reply to your recent inquiry
we do have the Elsie cow pitcher
this sells for $1.25 postpaid
shall be glad to ship this to
upon receipt of your check or
...ey order.

Yours very truly,

MALCOLM'S
HOUSE & GARDEN STORE

BALTIMORE, MD.
6·30PM

UNITED STATES
POSTAGE
1 CENT 1

Lucy E. Flint

24 Byrd Road

Wethersfield,

Connecticut

As we came
into the city
I should say
it was not
as pretty as the
card ...

East H...
Con...

Greetings FROM BALTIMORE MD.

2

GREETINGS from BALTIMORE

13276

Greater Baltimore, Baltimore, Md.

Postcard Views of the City

BERT SMITH

WITH A FOREWORD BY JACQUES KELLY

The Johns Hopkins University Press

Baltimore and London

A Robert G. Merrick Edition

© 1996 The Johns Hopkins University Press
All rights reserved. Published 1996
Printed in Hong Kong on acid-free paper
9 8 7 6 5 4 3 2

The Johns Hopkins University Press
2715 North Charles Street
Baltimore, Maryland 21218-4363
www.press.jhu.edu

The postcard of Memorial Stadium, fig. 89,
© D. E. Traub, is reprinted here with permission
of the owner.

All postcards in this book are from the collection
of the author, with the exception of figs. 99 and
100, which appear here with the kind permission
of the B&O Transportation Museum Library.

ISBN 0-8018-5534-9
LC 96-77688

To Anthea, who continues to inspire me

CONTENTS

FOREWORD

One of my favorite Baltimore postcards is addressed to a Julia Fowler, who lived on Myrtle Avenue in West Baltimore. The card is postmarked August 3, 1906. It depicts the old Hochschild, Kohn & Co. department store and has a space large enough for a message—five short sentences penned in a fine, clear hand.

"Dear Julia: Are you going down town tomorrow afternoon (Sat.)? If so, please meet me at Stewart's music dept. about 3:15. I expect to go down any way, so if you can not go you need not phone. How are you? I wanted to come over today but it was too hot. Lovingly, Edna."

Why use the telephone when you could drop a line via the mail carrier?

Our delight and fascination with antique postcards just will not quit. Visit one of Maryland's flea markets or ephemera shows. The crowd may casually wander past the tables piled with wares, but there will be a clutch of intent lookers huddled around the postcard table.

And as many times as I've spent a half hour browsing through trays of cards that once made their way to the Myrtle Avenues of Baltimore, I often still turn up a new find, a scene of Baltimore unknown to me. Just when you think you've seen every card there is, six more turn up. Many unusual finds are on the pages of this book.

Baltimore is a place where we cling to our traditions. We still issue our own postcards. Consider this business lineage:

The brothers Isaac and Mose Ottenheimer founded a firm in 1890. It didn't take long before they began selling thousands of cards bearing their imprint. Allan Hirsh Jr., grandson of Isaac, remains in the publishing business today. His catalog includes children's, cooking, and reference books. What he loves to talk about are the 3,000 different postcard scenes he and his family before him offered throughout Baltimore, Maryland, and Washington.

In 1952 Mr. Hirsh sold his postcard line to David Traub, who has continued to publish cards, along with other Baltimore souvenirs—the plastic crabs and snow domes that visitors carry home from the Inner Harbor.

The Traub firm remains in business today. Its busy, postcard-packed warehouse in the Remington neighborhood, just across the Jones Falls Valley from two favorite postcard-photographer destinations, Druid Hill Park and the Baltimore Zoo, is an easy walk from the home of the author of this book. Things just happen to work out that way in Baltimore.

JACQUES KELLY

ACKNOWLEDGMENTS

This project would not have been possible without the help and support of many people. First and foremost, my thanks go to my colleagues in the School of Communications Design at the University of Baltimore, Dr. Stephen Matanle and Dr. Neil Kleinman, for believing in my idea and helping me to make it a reality, and to all the other members of my division who offered support and listened when work was going less than smoothly. Thanks are also due to Prof. Jim Astrachan for his valuable advice and explanations, to Prof. Randall Beirne, whose information and personal knowledge of the military history of Maryland were invaluable, and to Baltimore historian and columnist Jacques Kelly for his encouragement and helpful comments.

Several people who helped me find the most interesting postcards for this book deserve credit and my thanks: Bill Martin, Mary Martin, and Paul Russell, who gave me special access to the wonderful stock of cards at their shop, Mary Martin Ltd., in Perryville; John Corliss, Marcella Lorden, and the rest of the Monumental Postcard Club members; Sunny and Wade Rice at the Wishbone in Silver Spring; and Shirley Stonesifer at Memory Lane in Keymar.

Debra Gust at the Curt Teich Postcard Archives in Wauconda, Illinois, showed me how to crack the date code and provided verification of dates on several cards. Anne Calhoun, librarian/archivist at the B&O Transportation Museum, kindly lent two postcards from the B&O collection. Norman Watkins supplied his expertise in photographing the cards, and when I was researching facts for the text, the librarians in the Maryland Room of the Enoch Pratt Free Library proved extremely valuable. Eric Agner skillfully set the type and fit pages together and managed to do both elegantly.

The people at the Johns Hopkins University Press have been enormously helpful in applying their professional skills to this book: Susan Ventura and Inger Forland in marketing; Julie McCarthy in manuscript editing; Anita Walker Scott, manager of design and production, whose patience and advice are greatly appreciated; and especially Robert J. Brugger, whose editorial wisdom and encouragement extracted pages of copy from me on the tightest of schedules.

Finally, my deepest appreciation and thanks go to the best editor, wordsmith, and friend I know—my wife, Anthea.

INTRODUCTION

Old postcards make us smile. We see their hand-painted scenes and faint postmarks and imagine the people who sent them. For a moment, we enjoy a connection to these travelers of other times and places we have never seen. If the pictures are of a place we've visited or known intimately, we're hooked; we want to see more. And there are thousands more to satisfy our appetite.

Picture postcards began in Europe in the late nineteenth century and by 1902 had spread to America. Three years later, people here were eager to buy three for a penny and mail them for a penny apiece—half the cost of paper, envelope, and postage for a letter—and they began to collect cards by the hundreds and save them in albums. At first restricted to writing only the address across the back, tourists and collectors wrote their names in a small white panel on the front or sometimes wrote a longer message right over the image. That all changed in 1907 when the post office permitted both address and message on the back. The craze built to a frenzy, and the "golden age" of postcards in America began.

Today, interest in these old cards has revived and intensified. Collected here are some of the best examples of Baltimore subjects. The earliest show the city just as it was recovering from the Great Fire of 1904, which destroyed twenty-four blocks of downtown. Then, and for fifty years afterward, postcards were printed from hand-painted versions of black-and-white photographs. At first they appeared in soft, delicate colors, but artists soon discovered that they could add a bright orange sunset—or make it

"midnight" by painting an inky sky and putting glowing yellow lights in all the windows. Some of the most sought-after cards then and now were individually hand colored *after* printing by anonymous workers who applied watercolor in an assembly-line process. (Several of these cards are included here.)

In the 1930s the colors got brighter and the age of "linens" began. Named for the imitation texture of the paper on which they were printed, these cards present idealized sunny views with bright green grass, red flowers, garish pink or deep blue skies, and cool purple shadows. Any visual clutter, like stray telephone poles, the odd pedestrian, or the rest of the entire neighborhood, simply disappeared by airbrush. To a generation jaded by flashy computerized

12184
Scene after the Great Fire, Baltimore, Md.

special effects, this tampering with reality might seem quaint and unremarkable, but back then linens were simply fun to look at. They still are.

Creatively colored and not simply reproduced from photographs, old postcards are genuine pieces of American folk art. More than that, they are reminders of a world that no longer exists. Many sites shown in this book, like the distinctively

Victorian old Post Office, are long gone, and the city is poorer for their loss. Others, like Camden Station and the B&O station, have been skillfully resurrected and adapted to new uses.

The cards appear here slightly oversize to bring out the details and make it easier to read signs, see the people and cars, and enjoy the view. So, whether you have deep roots in this wonderful city or are visiting it for the first time, I bring you *Greetings from Baltimore*.

BERT SMITH

This view (5) of part of the ruins of the Great Baltimore Fire of February 1904 shows the Hopkins Place Savings Bank still standing in the center. A little more than one year later, the bank (6) reopened within the same granite walls.

6

7

☆ GREETINGS from ☆

BALTIMORE

MD.

OB-H558

The Susquehanna, Baltimore, Md.

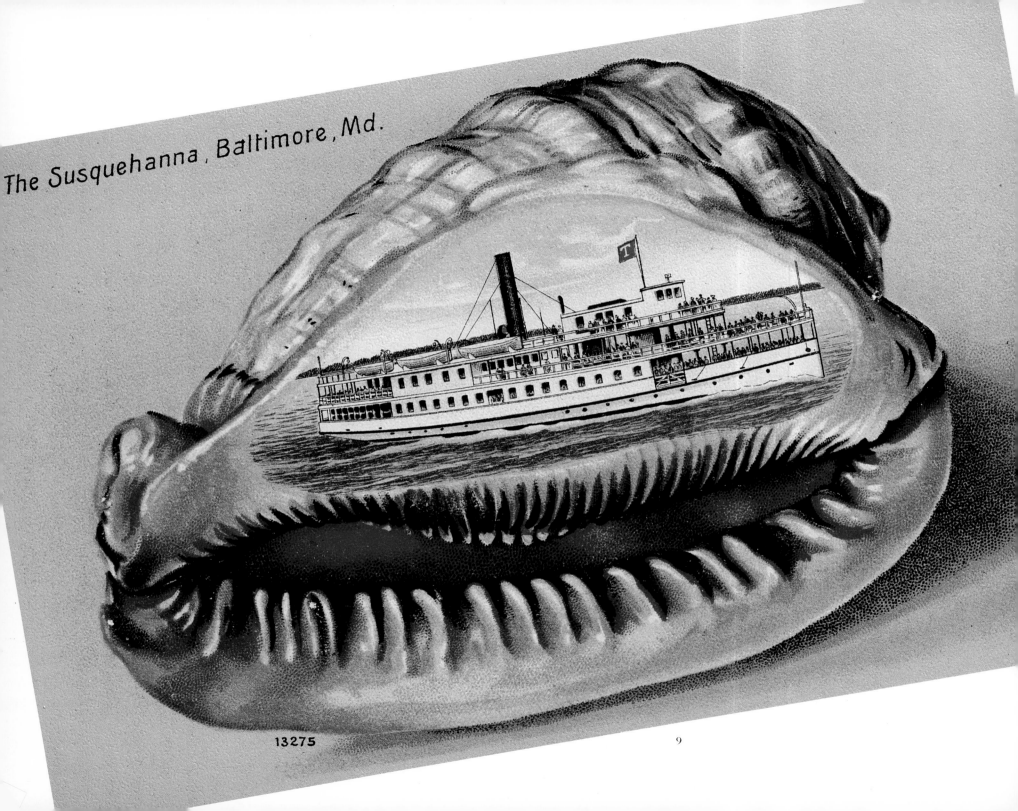

13275

9

The Harbor in the Age of Sail and Steam

The heart of Baltimore has always been its deep and well-protected harbor. First noted and mapped by Capt. John Smith in the journal of his 1608 voyage, the harbor has given shelter and opportunity to settlers who have come in waves ever since. The Susquehannock Indians lived to the north and hunted black bear and smaller game here; they fished these waters for hundreds, and perhaps thousands, of years. The river and the huge bay it flows into form a natural harbor that once was alive with mussels, crabs, oysters, and many kinds of fish. Piscataways had named the river the Patapsco and the bay the Chesapeake, meaning "great shellfish bay."

Harbor Entrance, from Fort McHenry.   BALTIMORE, Md.

10

Harbor, from Federal Hill.

Baltimore, Md.

Steaming within an embossed and finely printed shell from about 1908, the Susquehanna (9) was built in 1898 and sold to outside interests in 1923. She later returned to Baltimore as the Francis Scott Key. The harbor (10, 11) seems far from crowded in these delicately hand colored views that appeared starting about 1910.

11

After the first English colonists landed in southern Maryland in 1634, the tobacco they grew was packed in great wooden barrels called hogsheads and rolled from the outlying farms and plantations up and down the bay to the water for shipment to England. The harbor became one of the favorite shipping points for this commodity until well into the twentieth century.

Baltimore Town was established in 1729 and by 1745 had absorbed several smaller towns on either side of the Jones Falls. Named for the Irish home of the Calvert family, the lords Baltimore, who governed the colony for King Charles I, Baltimore expanded and remained quiet but increasingly cosmopolitan. It was not until after the Revolutionary War that the town grew into a city and a major port.

By the time it became a chartered city in 1797, Baltimore had become a center of shipbuilding. Its famous clippers raced from Baltimore to the Caribbean and Europe with cargoes of tea, spices, and silks. In that year, the *Constellation,* one of the first two ships of the young United States navy, was built at Fells Point, while in Boston its sister ship, the *Constitution,* was built to identical specifications. Both were to play important roles in the country's "second war of independence" from Britain, between 1812 and 1814.

The first steamboat appeared on the bay in the middle year of that war. Fittingly named the *Chesapeake,* she made the first run from Baltimore to Annapolis and back in

Steamer "Dreamland" on the Chesapeake Bay from Baltimore Md.

12

13

111366

SALOON OF FERRY STEAMER GOVERNOR ALBERT C. RITCHIE.

VIEW OF HARBOR, SHOWING EXCURSION BOATS, BALTIMORE, MD.

14

STEAMER "EXPRESS", BALTIMORE'S LARGEST EXCURSION STEAMER, BALTIMORE, MD.

15

107110

TB-8—Steamer Tolchester, Baltimore, Md.

16

The Dreamland (12) went to Chesapeake Beach from 1909 to 1925; one sat in wicker chairs in the saloon and enjoyed conversation (13). Often called Baltimore's favorite steamer, the Louise (14) ran to Tolchester for forty-two years before being replaced by the Express (15), which made the trips during 1925–33. Beginning in 1948, the newer Tolchester (16) ran for another seven years, ending her service in 1955.

17

Docks Baltimore, Md.

Baltimore looking down from Federal Hill.

Baltimore,

18

Standard Oil Co.'s Pier, Federal Hill in the distance.   BALTIMORE, Md.

19

The sidewheeler Avalon departs in the background (17). The view from Federal Hill (18)
looks to the northeast in about 1909. Typical of
growth around the harbor after the fire, the
Standard Oil Company's Pier takes shape about
1911 (19). Lazaretto Lighthouse (20) stood on a
point of the same name across the Patapsco
from Fort McHenry. Fresh oysters are being
loaded into wagons headed for market (21)
after a hard day working on the bay.

Baltimore, Md.

Lazaretto Light House.

9252. UNLOADING OYSTER LUGGERS BALTIMORE, MD.

COPYRIGHT
1905,
BY DETROIT
PUBLISHING
CO.

21

one day, for which her passengers paid a dollar each way. Following that success, other ships were built, and several small companies formed to compete with the sailing vessels then plying the bay.

The most famous and successful company of all, the Baltimore Steam Packet Company, emerged in 1840. Better known as the Old Bay Line, it scheduled the *City of Norfolk* and *City of Richmond* on overnight runs to Norfolk, Old Point Comfort, Portsmouth, and Richmond—as did its competitor, the Chesapeake Line. In 1844, the Ericsson Line began a route from Baltimore to the top of the bay and through the new Chesapeake and Delaware canal to Philadelphia. Later, ships of the Merchants and Miners Transportation Company went to Philadelphia and Boston, and the Baltimore Mail Steamship Line began making regular runs to LeHavre, France.

By the first decade of this century, boats from these and many smaller steamship lines crowded Baltimore's harbor. Businessmen, landowners, and mothers with young children found this a quiet and dignified way to travel. It was slow, but before World War II hardly anybody was in a hurry.

There was a genteel routine to these trips, which lasted until the early 1960s. Passengers for the night run down the bay to Norfolk and other points south boarded a steamboat at Pratt and Light streets, the city's busiest intersection, at the 4:30 departure time. After being shown to their carpeted stateroom, travelers might choose to walk around the deck on a warm summer evening, the smell of the water mixing with the pleasant aroma of spices from the McCormick plant just across Light Street. Following a blast from the whistle, the steamer would back out into the harbor, turn about, and move slowly down the Patapsco. Soon, a white-coated waiter appeared, ringing a handbell, and announcing that dinner was being served.

Around sunset, with dinner over, almost everyone would sit in deck chairs and watch Annapolis slip quietly by. As darkness approached, the lights of other boats could be seen across the water. This all began to disappear in the 1950s, as people found it easier to own their own cars and drive themselves. By 1959 the Old Bay Line carried only a few passengers each weekday, and in 1962 it ceased to operate.

In the warmer months of spring and summer, there were excursions to Tolchester, Betterton, Chesapeake, and Bay Ridge beaches. In the days before air conditioning, Baltimoreans looked forward to these inexpensive day trips as a cool escape on the water.

22

Widened considerably after the Great Fire (22), Light Street rolls down to the Old Bay Line's tower, clearly visible to the right of center. Steam still reigns as king in this 1940 view of the Pratt and Light street wharves (23). An early and unusual folding card (24) with a view north from Federal Hill in about 1906.

Baltimore Upper Harbor, Baltimore, Md.

23

24

View from Federal Hill, Baltimore, Md.

SUN COMPANY.

9

BIRDSEYE VIEW OF BALTIMORE AND CITY HALL.

25

Work and Play Downtown

In 1900 Baltimore was third among American cities in volume of foreign trade. Raw materials of every kind arrived in port. Manufactured products like toys, clothes, cotton duck and other textiles, canned goods, liquor, boots, and shoes left by water and rail daily in all directions. In fact, so many straw hats were made here in the 1920s (every proper gentleman owned at least one) that Baltimore was known as the straw hat capital of the world. Railroads kept foundries and machine shops busy. Steel rails were made at Sparrows Point.

The city grew as a financial center as well. With a population of more than half a million in 1900, Baltimore could boast of many savings banks into which a person of modest means could put a little money each payday and perhaps get a mortgage loan on a small rowhouse. Investment and other large banking firms grew downtown, along with private and business insurance companies, wholesalers, and commission merchants.

To the average Baltimorean this meant that work was almost always available, and, even if wages were low, housing was affordable and food was cheap. Life was good. In the four decades after the Civil War, immigrants arrived at Locust

These "birdseye" views (25) were popular in the years just following the Wright brothers' first flight. The McCormick Building (26) went up in a restrained deco style in 1921 (the company sold the building and it was razed in 1989). The Recreation Pier (27), now recognizable by viewers across the country as the police headquarters in the popular television series Homicide, appears as it looked in about 1910.

26

McCORMICK BUILDING, LIGHT BARRE AND CHARLES STREETS, BALTIMORE, MD.

98590

27

11 Recreation Pier, Foot of Broadway, Baltimore, Md.

3410

Point almost daily, eventually making it second only to Ellis Island in the number of newcomers who passed through its gates. Following on the heels of a large German population, Irish, Czechoslovakian, Russian, Italian, and Polish as well as Lithuanian and Greek peoples arrived to live side by side. African Americans from the Deep South as well as displaced farmers from Appalachia have worked in Baltimore's mills, factories, stores, and offices.

"Night views," such as this one of City Hall (28) circa 1940, allowed imaginative use of color. A standard blue sky and light clouds have been masked into an otherwise grey view of the courthouse (29) as it looked around 1922.

The wide-angle view of the old Post Office (30) dates from 1909. A hand-colored card of the Greek temple building of the Savings Bank of Baltimore (31) has special value because it also depicts streetcars. Brand new in 1906, the B&O Railroad's headquarters building (32) replaced the structure destroyed in the 1904 fire.

Night View of Baltimore, Md.

28

COURT HOUSE AND BATTLE MONUMENT, BALTIMORE, MD.

29

Post Office. Baltimore, Md.

30

32

9334. New B. & O. Building. Cr. Baltimore & No. Charles St., Baltimore, Md.

31

THE SAVINGS BANK OF BALTIMORE. BALTIMORE, MD.

13

ℬaltimore Street

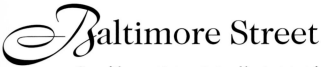

One of the most interesting and busiest stretches of downtown, Baltimore Street on either side of Charles Street always has been the center of the city. This intersection marks the beginning of all street numbers running east and west, north and south. Buildings on both sides stood directly in the path of the 1904 fire, and almost every one was completely destroyed. In the rebuilding that followed, the west side spawned offices, factory lofts, and small shops that made thousands of shirts, hats, handkerchiefs, suits, and other articles of clothing. At street level were retail stores and small businesses. East of Charles Street, however, things developed differently. A three-block section of Baltimore Street rose from the ashes and defined itself as an entertainment spot. Known all over the world as "the Block," this section became Baltimore's version of New York's 42nd Street or San Francisco's Tenderloin district. Top quality vaudeville acts appeared here, as did famous burlesque stars before the sleazier striptease, go-go dancers, tattoo parlors, and adult bookstores replaced them. In the 1920s and early 1930s, a Coney Island atmosphere of street vendors, 24-hour lunchrooms, and electric signs attracted people night and day. Beer cost ten cents a glass, the Victoria offered Yiddish theater, and there were several movie houses.

In the 400 block was the Gayety, the city's top burlesque house from the 1920s until a fire in 1969 forced it to close. Comedians—Red Skelton, Jackie Gleason, Phil Silvers, and "Pigmeat" Markham among them—and strippers appeared on its stage. The biggest names in striptease, or

"beauty flashing" as the management of the Gayety called it, performed there. Sally Rand, Gypsy Rose Lee, Ann Corio, Blaze Starr, Valerie Parks, Patti Waggin, Peaches, and Georgia Southern were some of the best known.

In the late 1960s and early 1970s, the Block fell apart under increasing police pressure. "Massage parlors" began cropping up, and many of the older establishments folded. Today, the plastic signs and guarded entrances are colder and raunchier, and now the Block is only one block long.

In 1909 the first two blocks west of Charles Street (33) were not as colorful as those on the east side. Although not specifically named here, "the Block" (34) is depicted as it looked in 1922, at about the time the Gayety Theatre, just left of center, became a top burlesque showplace. There are no known postcards of this area at night. The Gayety (35) was brand-new when this card appeared in 1906. A wonderfully clear bird's eye view (36) looks farther east toward Highlandtown in 1909.

34

BALTIMORE STREET, LOOKING WEST, BALTIMORE, MD.

35

86
Gayety
Theatr
Baltim
Md.

Baltimore, Md. Baltimore St. from Holliday St. looking East

36

15

Survivors

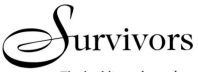

The buildings shown here are among Baltimore's most historic and architecturally significant. Survivors of many decades, they are all within easy reach of the Inner Harbor.

World renowned as a teaching hospital since it opened in 1889, Johns Hopkins Hospital, together with the medical school, is part of the university of the same name. Today, a huge complex of modern buildings surrounds these famous Victorians, and the hospital continues to stand at the leading edge of medical knowledge and practice.

Completed in 1821 as the first Roman Catholic basilica in America, the Basilica of the Assumption served as the seat of the first American bishop of that faith, John Carroll of Baltimore.

The University of Maryland's Davidge Hall, with its plain Greek Revival styling, stands at Lombard and Greene streets. Built in 1812 and the oldest medical school building in America, it once had to be protected from a mob who objected to the practice of cutting up cadavers for purposes of teaching.

A typical small dwelling of the early 1800s, the Flag House was the home of Mary Young Pickersgill, who sewed the 30' x 42' flag that flew over Fort McHenry in September 1814 and inspired Francis Scott Key to write the "Star-Spangled Banner."

Built in 1856, Old St. Paul's Episcopal Church at Charles and Saratoga streets contains a Louis Comfort Tiffany window in the chancel. Organized in 1692, it is the oldest church in Baltimore.

37

JOHN HOPKINS HOSPITAL, NORTH BROADWAY, BALTIMORE, MD.

38

The Cathedral.

Baltimore, Md.

39

40

41

St. Paul's Episcopal Church.

Baltimore, Md.

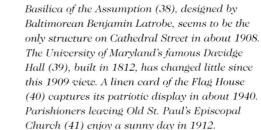

The original buildings of Johns Hopkins Hospital (37) stand out against a colorful sky in 1920. The Basilica of the Assumption (38), designed by Baltimorean Benjamin Latrobe, seems to be the only structure on Cathedral Street in about 1908. The University of Maryland's famous Davidge Hall (39), built in 1812, has changed little since this 1909 view. A linen card of the Flag House (40) captures its patriotic display in about 1940. Parishioners leaving Old St. Paul's Episcopal Church (41) enjoy a sunny day in 1912.

42

FLOWER MARKET, WOMEN'S CIVIC LEAGUE, WASHINGTON MONUMENT

43

Mount Vernon Place, Baltimore, Md.

Washington Monument at Night, Baltimore, Md.

Nighttime floodlighting of the Washington Monument (42), as seen here in 1940, continues today. The first Wednesday in May welcomes spring with the Flower Mart (43). With but few cancellations since its inception in 1911, the event still appears much as it did in this scene from about 1925.

44

The Washington Monument

Rising as the first urban monument to our first president (and long a symbol of the city), the Washington Monument in Mount Vernon Place was begun in 1815 on land donated by Revolutionary War hero John Eager Howard. It faces the harbor and took fourteen years to build.

Due to lack of funds, the original design had to be simplified several times, but in 1829, with much ceremony, the sixteen-ton marble statue capped the elegant column. The iron railing and interior details were not completed until 1842.

The monument is built to a design by Robert Mills, a student of both Thomas Jefferson and Benjamin Latrobe. He submitted it in a contest in 1813 and was chosen the winner. At the time, the monument's 178-foot-tall column was considered an engineering feat of the first order. The surrounding park soon became an elegant residential neighborhood that still contains some of the city's finest houses.

In 1911 the Women's Civic League held the first Flower Mart at the base of the monument. Now a fond Baltimore tradition, the Mart continues to feature booths from almost every city neighborhood, green plants for sale, and famous lemon peppermint sticks.

GER HOWARD STATUE AND WASHINGTON MONUMENT,
ORE, MD.

45

WASHINGTON AND
S. TEACKLE WALLIS MONUMENTS,
BALTIMORE, MD.

46

An eerily unpeopled Monument Square (44) dates from about 1909. In the same year, a sky never supplied by nature lights up this view (45). Ten years into the new century, two well-dressed women stroll through the park (46) between Monument and Centre streets.

19

Monuments to Other Heroes

Baltimore's monuments display a wide variety of stylistic influences and remind us of the city's proud record in every war since the Revolution.

The Francis Scott Key Monument, located in the 1300 block of Eutaw Place, portrays the author of the "Star-Spangled Banner" standing in a rowboat.

Erected in 1901, the Revolutionary War Monument rises almost sixty feet above the intersection of Mount Royal Avenue and Cathedral Street. Also called the "Maryland Line Monument," it honors troops of the same name who saved Washington's army in a heroic stand at Long Island in 1776.

A white obelisk erected in 1873 in Ashland Square on East Monument Street marks the final resting place of two Baltimore teenagers who were responsible for slowing the British advance at the Battle of North Point. In September 1814, nineteen-year-old Daniel Wells and eighteen-year-old Henry McComas shot and killed the British commanding general. Return fire from the British troops instantly killed the two young riflemen.

The Battle Monument in Court Square on Calvert Street makes an important democratic statement. Contrary to the custom of the day of noting only the commander, this monument honors and names all thirty-six soldiers killed at the Battle of North Point. It was erected in 1815, causing Baltimore to be known as "the monumental city."

A bronze statue of Lt. Col. William F. Watson, who was killed at Monterey, Mexico, in 1846, stands atop his monument, now moved to the end of Mount Royal Avenue at North Avenue.

Francis Scott Key Monument, Baltimore, Md.

Revolutionary Monument, Mt. Royal Station, Baltimore, Md.

This finely colored linen of the Francis Scott Key Monument (47) dates from about 1940. With its detail and magnificent sunset (48), this card from 1910 brilliantly celebrates the Mount Royal Avenue monument to Maryland's role in the Revolutionary War. More notable for its background of neatly shuttered houses than for the rather plain tribute (49) to the daring teenagers Wells and McComas, this card survives from about 1909.

12198 – Watson Monument, Baltimore, Md.

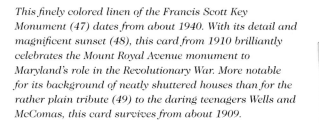

Battle Monument, Baltimore, Md.

Wells and Mc. Comas Monument, Ashland S

50

An unusual view of the Battle Monument in Court Square (50) has warm colors, an authentic yellow streetcar, and a postmark from 1942. The houses along Mount Royal Avenue in 1906 add interest to the image of Lt. Col. Watson's monument (51).

52

Shot Tower, East Fayette Street, Baltimore, Md.

The Shot Tower

One of only three such structures surviving in the country, the Shot Tower soars above the intersection of Front and Fayette streets, where it has stood since 1828. This remarkable piece of brickwork rose to completion in less than six months without the aid of a scaffold. Originally named the Phoenix Shot Tower, and later Merchants Shot Tower, this unusual building stands over 215 feet tall, contains more than one million bricks, and has walls four-and-a-half-feet thick at the base.

In towers such as this (there were three others in town), molten lead was dropped through a screen at the top, forming droplets on the way down which fell into cold water at the bottom. Workers then removed and sorted the lead balls according to size. Hunters used the shot mostly for birds and small game.

In an April Fool's Day trick in 1829, Edgar Allan Poe proclaimed that a man would fly from the tower's top to Lazaretto Lighthouse; the man never appeared. However, in 1880, a man actually did leap from the top while holding onto a large umbrella, and he lived to tell the tale. Today, docents entertain visitors daily with these and other stories about the tower, now a part of the City Life Museums.

One of the earliest cards depicting Baltimore, this view of the Shot Tower (52) includes a street scene from 1906. The same streets (53) have been cleared of every object in this colorful 1934 linen.

53

Actually a sepia-toned photograph (54), this card shows a wonderful, painted advertisement for Lord Calvert Coffee around 1925. Cars actually did not come in these colors (55), but an anonymous artist made them that way about 1940.

54

55

Shot Tower.   Baltimore, Maryland   6

SHOT TOWER, FAYETTE AND FRONT STREETS, BALT

OLD SHOT TOWER, BALTIMORE, MARYLAND.

The Bromo-Seltzer Tower

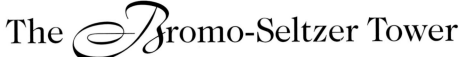

The pale yellow brick tower rising at the corner of Fayette and Eutaw streets survives as one of Baltimore's most readily identifiable landmarks. The lone survivor of the large factory and office structure originally attached to it, the tower came to life in 1911 as the brainchild of Capt. Isaac Emerson, founder of the drug company that bore his name. Bromo-Seltzer, the headache powder that came in a little cobalt blue bottle and cost ten cents, made the captain a millionaire twelve times over. Copied from the famous thirteenth-century Palazzo Vecchio in Florence, Italy, and displaying four clock faces larger than those of London's Big Ben, the Bromo-Seltzer Tower carried a metal replica of the blue bottle ten thousand times larger than the original. At night, the 596 electric lights embedded in its crown made the revolving fifty-one-foot-tall bottle visible for twenty miles. The blue bottle became closely identified with the city and survived until its removal in 1936. Today, with all but the ground floor closed to the public, the building serves as the Baltimore Arts Towers and stands as a highlight over the left field wall of Camden Yards.

BROMO-SELTZER TOWER BUILDING
LABORATORIES AND HOME OFFICE OF
EMERSON DRUG CO., BALTIMORE, MD.
COPYRIGHT 1911, BY EMERSON DRUG CO.

56

BUILDING, BALTIMORE, MD.

57

When its famous tower (56) was new in 1911, the Emerson Drug Company publicized itself with this card. All the activity in the street was painted in. Softer coloring appears in a view (57) from about the same time. The uniformed driver of this patient team and wagon (58) advertised the product all over town. A moody night scene (59) from the mid-twenties offers a good example of the dramatic effect that a creative postcard colorist could achieve. A later linen (60) has up-to-date cars and bold art deco color in 1935.

Bromo Seltzer Tower Building at Night,
North East Corner Eutaw and Lombard Streets.
Baltimore, Md.

59

58

EMERSON TOWER BUILDING,

60

NORTHEAST CORNER EUTAW AND LOMBARD STREETS, BALTIMORE, MD.

Shopping Downtown

Before World War II, people loved to shop downtown. No malls, no outlets, no golden arches kept them away, and the women arrived dressed for the occasion, wearing hats and gloves.

At Howard and Lexington streets, the May Company (later Hecht's) stood on the southwest corner. Before 1900, Samuel Hecht became the first city merchant to use price tags to curb price haggling. Across Lexington to the north, Hutzler's offered quality merchandise, a liberal return policy, and its famous balcony. Children delighted in Hutzler's holiday windows, Christmas gardens, and magical moving figures.

On the northeast corner, the more upscale Stewart's had a dazzling white facade and an art gallery that sold original paintings. Hochschild Kohn, which opened in 1897, stood on the southeast corner. Its success stemmed partly from "Bargain Friday," begun to attract farm families visiting nearby Lexington Market on that day. From 1936 to the mid-1960s, Hochschild's, like Macy's, sponsored its own Thanksgiving Toytown Parade. The Mickey Mouse, Cinderella, Goldilocks, and Noah's Ark balloons were maneuvered down Charles Street to the strains of "Here Comes Santa Claus."

Lexington Street packed in people six days a week with bargain stores, five-and-dimes, and small specialty shops. The hugely successful twelve-story Baltimore Bargain House took orders for wholesale clothing from near and far.

Today, only Hecht's remains as a reminder of these shopping traditions.

62

LEXINGTON STREET, WEST FROM PARK AVENUE, BALTIMORE, MD.

110190

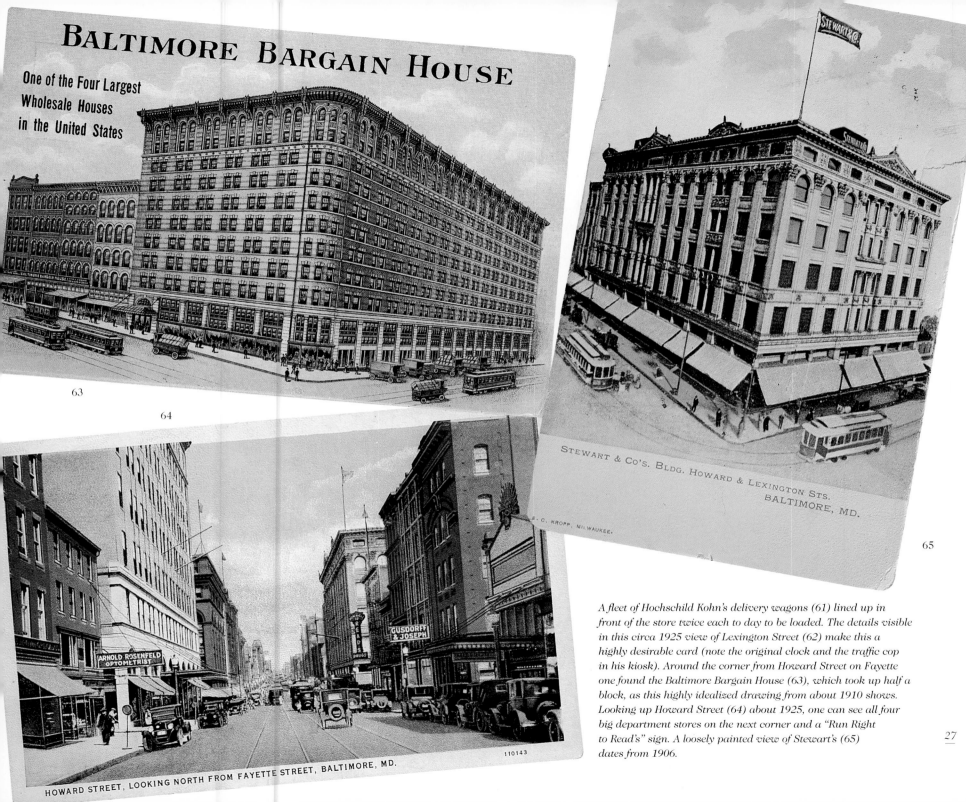

BALTIMORE BARGAIN HOUSE

One of the Four Largest
Wholesale Houses
in the United States

63

64

STEWART & CO'S. BLDG. HOWARD & LEXINGTON STS.
BALTIMORE, MD.

E. C. KROPP, MILWAUKEE.

GUSDORFF
& JOSEPH

ARNOLD ROSENFELD
OPTOMETRIST

110143

HOWARD STREET, LOOKING NORTH FROM FAYETTE STREET, BALTIMORE, MD.

65

A fleet of Hochschild Kohn's delivery wagons (61) lined up in
front of the store twice each to day to be loaded. The details visible
in this circa 1925 view of Lexington Street (62) make this a
highly desirable card (note the original clock and the traffic cop
in his kiosk). Around the corner from Howard Street on Fayette
one found the Baltimore Bargain House (63), which took up half a
block, as this highly idealized drawing from about 1910 shows.
Looking up Howard Street (64) about 1925, one can see all four
big department stores on the next corner and a "Run Right
to Read's" sign. A loosely painted view of Stewart's (65)
dates from 1906.

27

Lexington Market

The first small building erected in 1803 where Lexington Market stands today disappeared long ago, but the market actually traces its roots to 1782 and the days when farmers traded produce, cattle, and other commodities on the site.

The brick building that houses the stalls and counters of the present market dates from 1952 and replaced the old wooden structure that was destroyed by fire in March 1949. During demolition, the city also cleared away the outside stalls, which had become an unofficial part of the market scene.

Only a block from the old retail district at Howard and Lexington, the market has welcomed generations of browsers with their baskets and shopping bags looking for bargains in choice foods. Freshly butchered beef, pork, veal, and poultry, fruit from South America, fish, crabs, and oysters from the Chesapeake Bay, more exotic fare from the Atlantic, sandwiches, cut flowers, and gourmet candy are only a few of the hundreds of items that tempt today's buyers under one roof at this historic venue.

There have always been vendors outside as well as inside Lexington Market. This nicely hand colored card (66) bears a postmark of 1908. A wider view (67) shows the C. D. Kenny Company and a typically Baltimore row of brick buildings in mixed vintages and styles around 1910.

66

67

AT LEXINGTON MARKET.

BALTIMORE, MD.

HAND-COLORED

72063 LEXINGTON MARKET, BALTIMORE, MD.

Other Big Stores

The Montgomery Ward catalog house, the largest mercantile structure in the city when it opened in 1925, now stands empty at Monroe Street and Washington Boulevard. Once the center of the company's east coast operations, the eight-story building became the third busiest location in the pioneer mail order chain by 1955. Hutzler's Towson is notable as one of the earliest branch stores in the Baltimore area; it closed in 1990. Sears' stream-lined store on North Avenue at Harford Road closed after the civil disturbances of 1968.

Montgomery Ward's store (68) stands out vividly against a wild sky in about 1925. This card, from about 1952, celebrates Hutzler's sleek modern store in Towson (69), opened in that year. Sears' glass-fronted "super store" (70) opened in 1941, the year this card was printed. During the war years, artists often added American flags to views.

68

MONTGOMERY WARD CO. BUILDING, BALTIMORE, MD.

110004

TZLER'S TOWSON

Dulaney Valley and Joppa Roads
Baltimore County, Maryland

69

70

SEARS

...rd Company's New Super Store, Baltimore, Maryland

Druid Hill Park Lake, Skating, Baltimore, Md.

71

Sunday in the Park

In the days of the horse and carriage, when North Avenue was the northern boundary of the city, people who lived in town enjoyed driving out to Druid Hill Park to spend a day in the country-like surroundings. Or they took the horse-drawn streetcar to North Avenue and a hack the rest of the way to picnic and boat on the lake.

In the winter months, people came to skate on frozen Boat Lake, and many Sunday evenings saw the lake filled with a thousand skaters on the ice at one time. Refreshments were sold at the Mansion House and later at the house on the island known as the "Island Lodge," which also featured a warming fire in a small wood-burning stove.

Consisting of nearly seven hundred acres of trees and rolling grass lawns, Druid Hill is Baltimore's largest park. Established in 1860, it was occupied by Union troops who drilled and paraded there throughout the Civil War. Sheep calmly grazed its slopes from 1879 until 1945, when a shepherd could no longer be found.

To judge from postcards, Baltimore's lakes and streams stayed frozen for weeks at a time. The Boat Lake in Druid Hill Park (71) provided a popular skating site in about 1910. In summer, couples, as well as mothers with young children, could enjoy a walk around the lake (72), a stylish and wholly acceptable afternoon activity in 1906. Carefully colored, this 1909 card preserves an image of a fanciful Brightonesque bandstand (73) that no longer exists.

72

73

The oo

For many people in Baltimore, the zoo is the best part of a visit to Druid Hill Park. Second in seniority only to Philadelphia's, the Baltimore Zoo opened in 1876. At first little more than a small wild animal farm, it grew over the decades into a sophisticated collection of species.

A campaign by two mayors who made pleas for more than seven years to citizens and the Park Board finally resulted in the zoo securing its first elephant in 1925. Named Mary Ann, the elephant was shipped to Baltimore from India with the help of thousands of pennies donated by schoolchildren. She died in 1942 from injuries suffered in a fall. Minnie, who had been captured by Frank "Bring 'Em Back Alive" Buck in Siam, then became the star attraction, performing tricks with her trainer until her death in 1955.

Long before the Children's Zoo of the 1960s, Dr. Arthur Watson, the newly appointed director, opened a comical rabbit-sized village named "Bunnyville" in 1949 in an attempt to attract and entertain young visitors. Delighted children watched as rabbits "went to church," the "store," or their "homes" by entering variously labeled wooden constructions. Watson soon had families watching a half-hour television show called *This Is Your Zoo*. In perhaps his most successful publicity stunt, a finger-painting chimp named Betsy had her fifteen minutes of fame in the 1950s. Her local and national television appearances drew audiences of millions, some of whom bought her "art" and proudly displayed it in their homes and offices.

9352. Mansion House & Flock of sheep, Baltimore, Md.

74

Children Watching the Animals at Druid Hill Park Zoo, Baltimore, Md.

THIS PARK BELONGS TO YOU HELP KEEP IT CLEAN

75

ANIMAL HOUSE, DRUID HILL PARK, SHOWING MARY ANN, BALTIMORE, MD.

121245

76

77

BALTIMORE, MD.

Druid Hill Park,

"Mac," the shepherd, cannot be seen with his flock (74) in about 1906. The zoo has been the destination of school and church group outings for generations of Baltimoreans. Depression-era children are shown having a good time (75), despite being well chaperoned. Around that same period, Mary Ann (76), the star attraction at the elephant house, enjoys a meal. This sharply detailed and nicely colored view of the Bear Pit (77) from 1906 reveals not only the fancy dress of the day but also the conditions in which the bear lived.

Patterson Park and Clifton Park

Established in the early 1800s on land donated by William Patterson, father of Betsy, who married Jerome Bonaparte, the much-expanded Patterson Park on Eastern Avenue has many ties to Baltimore's history.

From the vantage point of Hampstead Hill, Baltimoreans set up cannon and breastworks in 1813 to defend the city from possible attack. The British delayed landing until the hill became a mustering point for local companies that were marching to the Battle of North Point.

In 1887, when electricity made possible concerts at night, questions of immoral behavior soon arose. The park's ten lamps hardly seemed to shed sufficient light to keep couples apart.

The Chinese Pagoda, erected in 1891 on Hampstead Hill as an observatory, still provides excellent views of the harbor, Locust Point, Canton, and on down to the bay. Repaired and repainted many times, the pagoda's color combinations have included green and white, orange and yellow, and maroon and cream.

In the northwest part of the city, philanthropist Johns Hopkins surrounded his Italianate mansion with trees, shrubs, and flowers until his death in 1873, twenty-two years before the area became Clifton Park. By 1916, a municipal golf course had been laid out in the park and a professional instructor hired. In addition, the park's swimming pool was the largest in the country. A version of the flower-filled memorial "Mother's Garden," created in 1926, remains in the park today.

79

Observatory, Patterson Park, Baltimore, Md.

8789   Clifton Park Swimming Pool, Baltimore, Md.

Baltimore, Md. Johns Hopkins Mansion, Clifton Park.

The enormous bandstand (78) in Patterson Park dominates
the hilltop in 1932. Swimming contests (79) and other activ-
ities kept children busy in the summer of 1929, just as they
do today. The Observatory (80), more commonly called the
Chinese Pagoda, awaits visitors with an open door in 1911.
In Clifton Park (81) in about 1930, young swimmers are
"shooting the chutes" into the shallow water. Philanthropist
Johns Hopkins left his mansion (82), Clifton, to the university that bears his name, with the house becoming the nucleus
of the present-day park and golf course. The artist for this
card (1910) made the shrubbery bloom full force.

Amusement Parks

The late nineteenth century has been called the Golden Age of parks in Baltimore. In addition to acreage set aside as quiet country settings in the city, other less tranquil parks flourished.

The arched and towered entrance of Electric Park, one of Baltimore's earliest amusement parks, lighted the night sky from the 1890s until 1916. Just inside, a crowded restaurant and bar beckoned the hungry for crab sandwiches and beer. Visitors marveled at the cyclorama of the Johnstown Flood. Young and old rode the carousel and roller coasters. The casino, under hundreds of colored lights, offered plays, rides, vaudeville acts, odd exhibits, and boxing matches. Spectators thrilled to cowboys and Indians in Pawnee Bill's Wild West Show, and the day often ended with Professor Pain's fireworks.

In 1894 the Powhattan Railroad opened Gwynn Oak Park on seventy-six acres at the end of its Woodlawn line. The park's lake, picnic grounds, band shell, and rides entertained Baltimoreans for generations. In the 1940s, visitors danced to big-name bands—Tommy Dorsey, Artie Shaw, and Glenn Miller among them—in the Dixie Ballroom.

"Report card day" in the 1950s, allowed free rides for any child presenting a passing report card. The Ferris Wheel, Wild Mouse, Caterpillar, and Big Dipper roller coaster competed with the Fun House, Penny Arcade, and Pistol Pete's Shooting Gallery for customers. But the fun ended in 1972 when tropical storm Agnes heavily damaged the park.

83

Electric Park At Night, Baltimore Md.

Dancing Pavilion, Gwynn Oak Park, Baltimore, Md.

84

85

86

BIRD'S-EYE VIEW AMUSEMENT SECTION CARLIN'S PARK. BALTIMORE, MD.

44451

A short ferry ride out of Baltimore, Bay Shore Park's concrete pier extended a thousand feet into the bay. Patrons enjoyed seafood suppers in the Colonial Dining Room and rides that included the Thing-A-Ma-Jig roller coaster, Skooter bumper cars, Toboggan water slide, and the Monkey Shine trolley line. The more adventurous took boat rides to a lighthouse three miles out. Bethlehem Steel later bought the property and dismantled the park.

For over forty years, the pagoda-like towers and Japanese gates of Carlin's Park at Park Circle welcomed visitors to enjoy the Racer Dip roller coaster, Fun House, Penny Arcade, olympic-size pool, and "Iceland," where the Clippers played until the mid-1950s. During the 1930s, the main attraction was the Dance Hall, site of dance marathons and the music of bands such as those of Paul Whiteman, Tex Benecke, and Duke Ellington. Rudolph Valentino caused a near riot when he danced there in 1923. Although the park survived a disastrous fire in 1932, all the rides had closed by 1955, and the ice rink closed a short time later.

Soon after the invention of the light bulb, sites like Electric Park (83) became all the rage. Re-created for the 1990 movie Avalon, *the real thing shines here in 1912. Probably the forerunner of the Dixie Ballroom, the Dancing Pavilion in Gwynn Oak Park (84) seems a much quieter venue in 1910. Bay Shore Park's restaurant pavilion (85) appears almost deserted in a 1916 view (note the price of supper). The gaudily colored scene (ca. 1940) of Carlin's Park (86) under a turquoise sky captures the fun of the place.*

The backs of postcards are often more interesting than the fronts because they share a moment from people's lives. A poignant message and the date and place from where the card was sent add interest for some collectors.

Blue Star Motel
WHITE MARSH, MARYLAND
U. S. Route #40 — 12 Miles North of Baltimore
Clean — Comfortable — Modern Rooms furnished with Beauty-rest Mattresses — Hot Water Heating — Private Baths
Owner & Manager: R. T. Webster
Phone: Chase—4584

K3075

A "Colourpictu

A great city, proud, self-sufficient, Baltimore sits beside the Patapsco River looking nostalgically south, but turning North for what it takes to make bank accounts grow. It is a city charmingly picturesque in its ugliness, yet seething with activity and opportunity.

Army 6   Navy 14
T. C. U. 7   S. M. U.
Miss. 13   Miss State 7
7   Vanderbilt 0
13   Oregon State 0
Everest
740 Puritan St
Balto.

11/27/41

BALTIMORE, MD.
NOV 28
12-M
1941

POST CARD

RED CROSS ROLL CALL JOIN

UNITED STATES POSTAGE

Wonder Football Contest
Radio Station
W.C.B.M
Balto.

POST CARD

MESSAGE MAY BE WRITTEN ON

BALTIMORE, MD.
AUG 15
3 PM
1922

As we came into the City, I shovel day it was not as pretty as the cord G. Mansur

august 4, 1950

Dear Helen,
I having a wonderful time. Got here about 12:30. Went shopping for two days & had a swell time. You should see the things I got. We watch television every night until 12; go to bed about 1 or 2; + get up 10 or 10:30. What a life! Nothing to do but sit around + relax. They have some swell westerns on television. We saw the Lone Ranger, Tim McCoy, Stop the music, + lots others. Everything doesn here is in a hurry, except me. Love — Lucille

BALTIMORE, MD.
AUG 5
12:30 PM
1950

POST CARD

Mrs. Helen Putman
Route 3
Frederick, Maryland

UNITED STATES POSTAGE
GEORGE WASHINGTON
1 CENT

Postcard 1 (top left):

The Excursion Steamers are very popular with the Natives of Baltimore. During the day many trips are enjoyed and from May to October, daily "Moonlight Rides" down the bay are crowded with happy merry-makers.

PUB. BY CALVERT NEWS CO., BALTIMORE, MD.

TICHNOR QUALITY VIEWS, REG. U.S. PAT. OFF., MADE ONLY BY TICHNOR BROS., INC., BOSTON, MASS.

Dear Mr Parks

My Name Miss Dolores Marx

Address - 2817 Berwick

Balto 14 Md

Phone Hamilton 7490

TV WAAM

Channel 13

BALTIMORE, MD
AUG 25
8-PM
1959

71003

Postcard 2 (top right):

POST CARD

MESSAGE MAY BE WRITTEN ON THIS SIDE — ADDRESS ONLY ON THIS SIDE

MOUNTAIN

MENUE CARD

20 PRUNES 10¢

OAT MEAL WHEN YOU CAN GET IT 20¢

VIRGINIA HAM NICE & TENDER 60¢

CHICKEN IN THE ROUGH AS YOU WANT IT #1.50

New York

PUBLISHED BY I. & M. OTTENHEIMER, BALTIMORE, MD., MADE IN U.S.A.

R-24429

BALTIMORE, MD
JUN 22
12-PM
1947

5-

UNITED STATES POSTAGE
1 CENT

Miss Anna Morr--
345 Smyser
Yor--

Postcard 3 (bottom left):

We are now booking orders for 1912

Packard Motor Cars.

Packard "30" Standard- $4200.

Packard "18"   "   - 3200.

Packard "Six" Cylinder- 5000.

Shipped on a schedule -Early deliveries. Order at once and secure choice of shipping dates. Particulars on request. Phone or write at once.

Mar-Del Mobile Co.

Baltimore.

160 PUBLISHED BY J. THOS. SMITH, BALTIMORE, MD., MADE IN U.S.A.

A-17651

BALTIMORE, MD
APR 22
1911

Mrs. L. Fah--

Hagers--

Postcard 4 (bottom right):

POST CARD

COMMUNICATION.

Published by J. Thos. Smith, Baltimore, Md."

Dear Mary, I am on my way to Chesapeake Beach on this grand boat having a good time dancing Love Edna

U.S. POSTAGE
ONE CENT

CHESAPEAKE BEACH
AUG 11
1 AM
1911
MD.

Miss Mary Horner

c/o Geo. Fitch.

Rossville

Balto. Co. M--

Box # 85-

The Stadium

Baltimore Stadium, Baltimore, Md.

87

THE BALTIMORE STADIUM, 33RD STREET BOULEVARD, BALTIMORE, MD.

The story of Baltimore Stadium is mostly one of football on the college and military-team level, but baseball figured prominently in its last ten years. Built in 1922 on top of a former brick quarry, the stadium hosted many Navy–Notre Dame contests, an occasional Maryland game, and several matches between teams like the Quantico Marines and Army Third Corps.

When old Oriole Park burned to the ground in the early morning of July 4, 1944, destroying the International League Orioles' home and all their records and trophies, Baltimore Stadium became a baseball park almost overnight. On that hastily built diamond, the Orioles played the rest of 1944 and all their remaining minor league seasons, winning the International League World Series in 1944 and 1945.

88

The classic Greek portico of the stadium (87) and its colonnade stood on 33rd Street from 1922 through 1953. This view dates from about 1932. Few empty seats appear in this 1944 aerial view (88), probably with a Navy–Notre Dame football game in progress. Here Memorial Stadium (89) awaits the next Colt game in the fall of 1954.

89

Through decades of wins and losses, Baltimore fans have supported a number of sports teams in various leagues, but nothing compares to the devotion shown to the Orioles and the Baltimore Colts at Memorial Stadium, newly built in 1954. Beginning that same year, the American League Orioles played their last game here in October 1991. The National Football League Colts, who began in 1953 and played thirty-one seasons here, will forever be identified with Baltimore and the stadium. After attending a Colt game in the 1950s, a New York sportswriter called Memorial Stadium "the world's largest outdoor insane asylum."

Like Camden Yards, the shiny new Memorial Stadium was set to be called Babe Ruth Stadium, but Gold Star Mothers and other organizations campaigned for a memorial to the war dead, and they won.

T is the star spangled banner
oh long may it wave,
O'er the land of the free
and the home of the brave.

90

"Oh Flag beloved
forever dear!
Oh Flag unstained
by sordid deeds
Wide spread thy folds
and gather safe,
The men of various
warring creeds."

Chapman

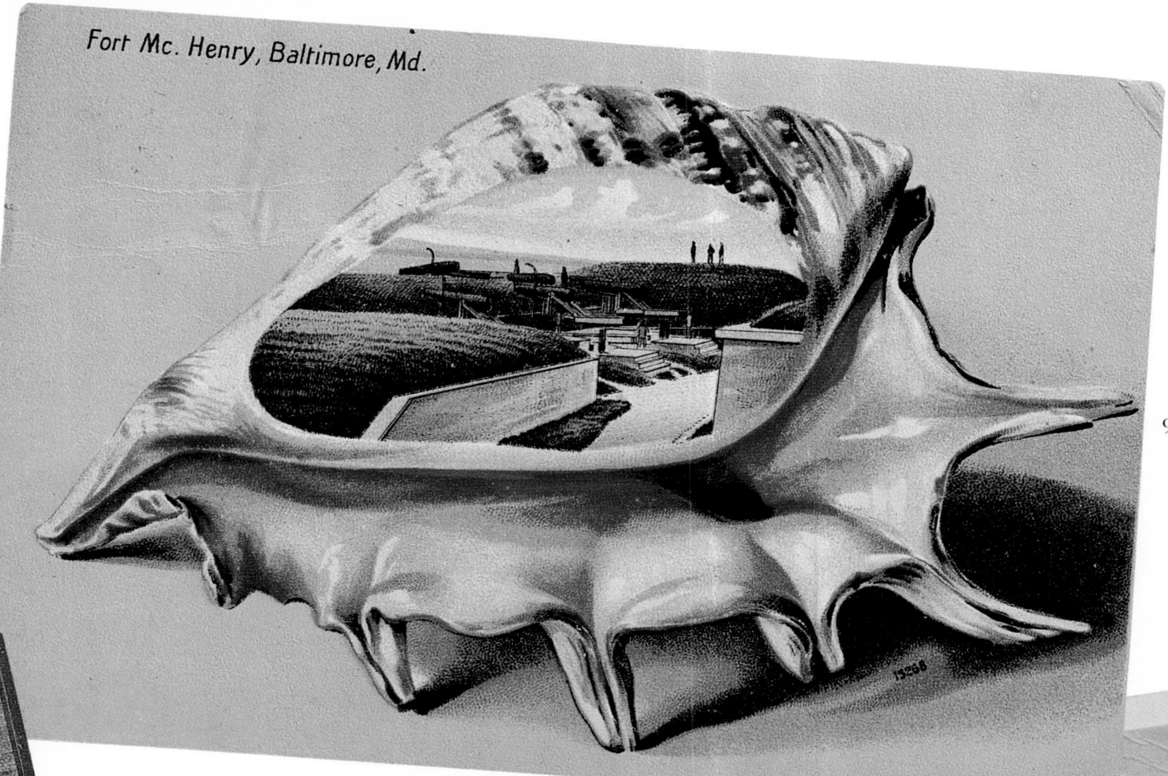

Fort Mc. Henry, Baltimore, Md.

91

THE HUMAN FLAG, FORT MC HENRY, STAR SPANGLED BANNER CELEBRATION, BALTIMORE, MD.

92

Patriotic displays such as this one (90) from about 1909 were common in Teddy Roosevelt's America. Civil War cannon (91) appear in a beautifully lithographed and embossed shell design from 1908. In a custom that continues today, schoolchildren form a human flag in this card (92), postmarked 1922. Marines guard the fort's entrance in a hand-colored card (93) from 1909. The colors are much brighter in a 1947 view (94) of visitors walking the grounds.

93

Fort McHenry. BALTIMORE, Md.

Home of the Star Spangled Banner, Fort McHenry, Baltimore, Md.

94

Fort McHenry

Of all the historical shrines in America, Fort McHenry holds a preeminent position, for here our national anthem came to life. A few lines of verse quickly penned by Francis Scott Key as he glimpsed the stars and stripes of the huge American flag still flying over the fort "by dawn's early light" on September 14, 1814, became the "Star-Spangled Banner."

Built to defend the Baltimore harbor in 1776, the original earthworks on this spot never saw action in the Revolutionary War, but they did keep British cruisers from harming the city. Completely redesigned between 1798 and 1800, the star-shaped-fort we see today took its name from Marylander James McHenry, then secretary of war. Then in 1814, after the British attacked and burned most of Washington and headed for Baltimore, the small fort stood in their path. Its inspirational defense of the city demoralized British forces and proved that the young nation was determined to stay free.

Union artillery occupied the fort during the Civil War, but they were never fired upon. The cannon a visitor sees today are the ones they left behind. The fort was deactivated in 1912 and now serves as a National Historic Monument.

The flag that survived the historic bombardment is today dramatically displayed in the National Museum of American History in Washington, D.C. Its unusual fifteen stars and fifteen stripes, correct in 1814, are sewn from the best material Mary Young Pickersgill could obtain—long-fibered wool bunting imported from England.

White Marble Steps

White Steps in Baltimore, Md.
(A familiar sight in older sections of the city.)

In the longest unbroken block of its kind in Baltimore, rowhouses march up Wilkens Avenue in about 1935. A set of white marble steps, a symbol of the city, receives its legendary once-a-week scrubbing from the woman at left.

The Greyhound Bus Station

Greyhound Bus Terminal, Baltimore, Md.

3B-H71

*One of many rising all over the country in the 1940s, a fine example
of a streamlined Greyhound bus station appears at Howard and Centre
streets. Still standing, now adapted for new use, it no longer serves as
a stop for nattily painted buses.*

America's First Railroad

A small group of concerned Baltimore business-men met in 1826 to decide what to do about the Erie Canal. Opened the year before in upstate New York, the canal threatened to put New York City far ahead of Baltimore in shipping goods westward to ever-expanding markets. The result was the Baltimore and Ohio Railroad, chartered by the state of Maryland in 1827.

The perfect spot to begin the railroad proved to be Mount Clare, and from this area of West Baltimore the first rails in America spread in all directions. Mount Clare Station, complet-ed in 1830 and still operating as part of the B&O Transportation Museum, can rightly boast of its distinction as the birthplace of American rail-roading. Mount Clare is the oldest railroad station in America, and probably the world.

Camden Station, built in sections between 1857 and 1867, and beautifully restored today as the main entrance to Oriole Park at Camden Yards, served as the B&O's first large passenger station. Lincoln actually passed through its gates three times: first, in the secretive overnight trip to his inauguration in 1861; second, on his way to Gettysburg to deliver the famous address three years later; and then, sadly, third, in 1865 when his body was taken off the train to lie in state in Baltimore on its slow ride to a final rest-ing place in Springfield, Illinois.

Among a long list of firsts for the B&O are being first to operate a locomotive, 1829; first dining car, 1843; first to reach the Mississippi River, 1857; and the first air-conditioned passenger car, 1930.

46

Camden Station, B. & O. Railroad, Camden & Howard streets, Baltimore, Md.

97

98

Baltimore, Md. Mount Royal Station

The William Crooks train, first to operate in the Northwest in 1861, on what is now a part of the Great Northern Railway, and the Blackfeet Indians of Glacier National Park and Waterton Lakes National Park, in attendance at the BALTIMORE AND OHIO RAILROAD'S FAIR OF THE IRON HORSE.

Camden Station (97) as it looked on a peaceful day in about 1918, long before it became part of a baseball park. In April 1861, Union troops marching toward Camden Station from the President Street Station ran afoul of a hostile mob, resulting in the first deaths of the Civil War. Mount Royal Station (98) enjoyed a reputation as a comfortable passenger terminal until it closed in 1958. A view from 1908 also shows some neat rowhouses on Bolton Hill. Today, following an award-winning renovation, Mount Royal serves as part of the Maryland Institute College of Art. Two black-and-white cards (99, 100) helped to celebrate the railroad's 1927 centennial. The Fair of the Iron Horse, drawing Indians from Montana and area schoolchildren as guests, featured old engines and a new President Line of locomotives. In 1911, rival Pennsylvania Railroad built the "New Union Station" (101), which is shown in 1922 as if painted by moonlight.

101

100

NEW UNION STATION BY NIGHT, BALTIMORE, MD.

Flying into Baltimore

By about 1920, Baltimore had a small airport called Logan Field on land bordering the Patapsco River southeast of the city. Adjacent to this early facility, newer and larger Municipal Airport served through the 1940s. In the mid-1930s, the nearby Glenn L. Martin plant had begun producing its famous Clipper, a large streamlined seaplane designed to carry passengers on international flights. In 1937, much to the delight of Baltimoreans, Pan American Airways began flying its fleet of Martin Clippers from this field.

Officially named Baltimore Municipal Airport in 1941, it became known as Harbor Field after the Second World War. The runways, however, proved too short to handle the latest commercial planes and planners began looking elsewhere to build a new state-of-the-art airport.

Officials looked as far as Anne Arundel county and, in June 1950, Friendship International Airport opened in grand style. President Truman spoke, the Marine band played, and adventurous visitors enjoyed free airplane rides throughout the day. As part of the festivities, the first international flight from the new, jet-age airport departed for Europe.

Although the airport was five times the size of Washington's National Airport and had the longest runways on the east coast, only nine airlines operated from its single pier that first year; at times the airport appeared deserted. Renamed Baltimore-Washington International Airport in 1973, it serves an ever-growing population from its bustling, modern and still-expanding facility.

102

Yankee Clipper, one of Pan American Airways' Transatlantic Planes, Entering its Hangar at the Baltimore Municipal Airport, Baltimore, Md.

49:-SEAPLANES AT BALTIMORE'S TRANSATLANTIC AIR BASE, MUNICIPAL AIRPORT, DUNDALK, NEAR BALTIMORE, MD.

47335

103

104

Largest Unit Aircraft Plant in the U.S.A.

9A-H1601

Co. Aircraft Plant, Middle River, near Baltimore, Md.

105

Main Lobby, Friendship Airport, Baltimore, Md.
Al Green Enterprises, of Maryland, Inc.

106

servation Ramp, Friendship Airport, Baltimore, Md.
Al Green Enterprises of Maryland, Inc.

Collectors prize postcards of airplanes, especially scenes before World War II. Photographed in about 1940, the Yankee Clipper (102) represented one of Pan Am's (and the Glenn L. Martin plant's) most famous planes. The giant seaplanes (103) float poised for action at Baltimore's largest airport in 1941. During the war, Glenn L. Martin (104) turned out thousands of bombers. In a card postmarked 1941, an imaginative artist airbrushed in a diving plane to enliven an otherwise dull view. Much fanfare accompanied the opening of Friendship Airport in 1950, but no one appears in this stark view of the main lobby (105) four years later. An outside view from the observation ramp (106) shows employees busily loading an Eastern Airlines plane before takeoff.

49

Public School No. 55. Hampden, Baltimore, Md.

107

School Days

By the 1860s, Baltimore was able to educate children through high school, but the largest growth in education occurred during the last quarter of the nineteenth century.

Public School No. 55 in Hampden exemplifies a successful public school that still thrives because it enjoys the support of caring teachers, parents, and community. Originally built in 1890 at Chestnut and Fourth avenues, it featured Victorian tin ceilings, beaded wainscoting, and marble lavatory floors. Until 1914, it was often called the "German school" because of classes held in German for the children of local millworkers who had moved from Pennsylvania. In 1979 a modern building replaced the old structure. A year later the state legislature recognized the school as one of the best of its kind in Maryland.

By the 1880s, most public schools were crowded and understaffed. For those parents who could afford the fees, the growing number of private schools in downtown Baltimore provided a solution. To help answer this need, B&O heiress Mary Garrett and her friends opened Bryn Mawr School for Girls in 1885 as a college preparatory school for girls who wished to attend good universities. The school moved to its present location in the early 1930s.

Children on the playground at Hampden Elementary School (107) in about 1910 enjoy freedom from the classroom. The Bryn Mawr School for Girls' (108) lovely brick building appears in a hand-colored view of about 1910, years before it served as the Deutsches Haus, a popular German restaurant with its own beer garden. It was eventually demolished to make way for the Meyerhoff Symphony Hall. In the same year, Public School No. 98 (109), also known as Samuel F. B. Morse Elementary, occupied a handsome four-story building.

108

109

High Schools

High school memories in Baltimore began with the four schools mentioned here.

City College, Baltimore's oldest public high school and the country's third oldest, opened in 1839 on Courtland Street as the "High School" for boys. Its name changed when it offered a first-year college curriculum. In 1875, City moved to Howard and Centre streets and provided an English and classical curriculum emphasizing Greek and Roman history, which changed to a more progressive curriculum by World War I.

The famous "A" course, designed to complete five years' work in four, began in 1926 with science, languages, and math. Two years later, the neo-Gothic "Castle on the Hill" opened. From the 1940s until the mid-1960s, special art and music curricula were added and in 1977, during restructuring as a school for the humanities, it became coed.

Following the opening of City, pressure built to open schools for girls. In 1844 eastern and Western High Schools began "in consideration of the delicacy of the females who wished to be educated." Girls of "good moral character" studied English, belles-lettres, mythology, philosophy, writing, and ornamental drawing. Classes lasted from 9 A.M. to 5 P.M. and August was the only vacation month.

Eastern opened at Front and Fayette streets, then moved to North Avenue and Broadway in 1906, and finally to 33rd Street in 1938. In 1986, Eastern merged with Lake Clifton High School. The building stands empty today.

29:-CITY COLLEGE. BALTIMORE. MD.

47323

New Eastern High School, Baltimore, Md.

8A-H1655

110

111

112

POLYTECHNIC INSTITUTE, NORTH AVE. & CALVERT ST., BALTIMORE, MD.

113

WESTERN HIGH SCHOOL, MCCULLOH STREET AND LAFAYETTE AVENUE, BALTIMORE, MD.

Western began on Paca Street with thirty-six girls, and required no written exams until 1855. In 1895, it moved to Lafayette Avenue and McCulloh Street, then to Gwynns Falls Parkway in 1928. Since 1967, it has shared the complex on Cold Spring Lane with the Polytechnic Institute.

For over a century, students interested in math, physics, and engineering have chosen the Polytechnic Institute. Opened in 1884 on the same street as City, the Boys Manual Training School became Poly in 1893. Six years later, with guidance from two Naval Academy officers, it became an engineering school to train young men in converting sailing vessels to steam power. Poly's own rigorous "A" course continues today, and despite recent attempts at reorganization and standardization, the school's reputation for academic excellence remains unsurpassed. Its former home on North Avenue—where H. L. Mencken studied—now houses the Baltimore Public School System administration.

Poly's rivalry with City in academics and sports is one of the oldest in the country, and for years their legendary football game was the highlight of Thanksgiving weekend. Today this classic is played as a regular season game.

A technicolor sky hangs over the "Castle on the Hill" (110) in a card from about 1932. Six years later, the same tower rises from behind the recently built Eastern High School (111). The building that any Baltimorean over the age of forty-five knows as Poly (112) had the grass lawns depicted when this card appeared about 1925. One of the many homes for Western (113), this view of the solid Romanesque revival structure dates from 1920.

MECHANICAL HALL, JOHNS HOPKINS UNIVERSITY, HOMEWOOD, BALTIMORE, MD.

114

69 State Normal School, Towson, Baltimore, Md.

5457

115

85:—GOUCHER COLLEGE, BALTIMORE, MD.

29005

116

Baltimore, Md. Maryland Institute.

117

Higher Education

Founded in 1876, the Johns Hopkins University pioneered use of the laboratory and seminar as vehicles for teaching. About 1905 the university left Howard Street for the grounds of Homewood, once owned by the son of Charles Carroll of Carrollton and now home to classrooms, laboratories, the Milton S. Eisenhower library, and NASA's Space Science Telescope Institute.

The State Normal School, known today as Towson State University, opened in 1866 in old Red Men's Hall on Paca Street. In 1915, the school left downtown for its current location on York Road. It was renamed Towson State Teacher's College in 1935 when it began offering a bachelor's degree.

Nationally recognized Goucher College provides its students with a broad background in the arts and sciences. Founded in 1888 as the Women's College of Baltimore and renamed for president Dr. John Goucher, it moved to Towson in the 1950s. Students in the 1960s were early demonstrators for racial equality but also invited George Wallace to speak. The college became coed in 1987.

The Maryland Institute College of Art began in 1826 as the Maryland Institute for the Promotion of the Mechanical Arts, with a technically oriented curriculum. After the 1904 fire destroyed the old Marsh Market Building, the school built its present Renaissance revival structure in 1907, funded largely by donations from Andrew Carnegie and other local patrons. Known today as one of the finest art schools in America,

Peabody Institute, Baltimore, Md.

118

its buildings include a former shoe factory and a railroad station.

Opened in 1868 as the Academy of Music and the first endowed institution of its kind, the Peabody Conservatory of Music on Mount Vernon Place has welcomed Tschaikovsky, Anton Rubenstein, Aaron Copland, Leonard Bernstein, and others to perform on its stage. International students benefit from teachers who excel at detecting and developing talent. The Peabody now forms part of the Johns Hopkins University.

Baltimore's continuing reputation as a center of culture and learning is due in large part to these institutions.

In a circa 1925 card picturing the Homewood campus of Johns Hopkins University, Gilman Hall displays its earlier name of Mechanical Hall (114). Another card from about the same time shows the State Normal School (115), better known today as Towson State University. In the latter, the artist added two cars, but the one on the left is comically out of scale. Goucher College (116) once graced St. Paul Street, close by Lovely Lane Methodist Church. In 1909 the white marble main building (117) of the Maryland Institute College of Art actually sparkled. A circa 1936 view of the Peabody Institute (118) features warm tones and a Renaissance perspective.

Orleans Street Viaduct

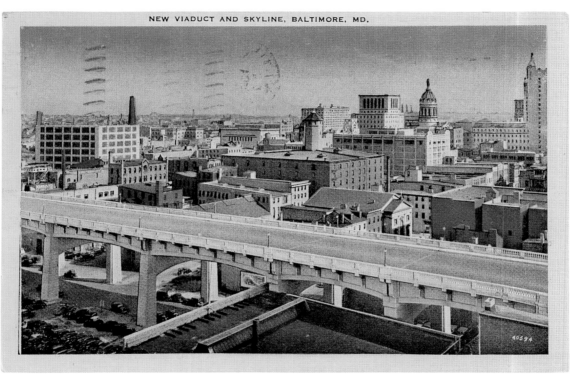

NEW VIADUCT AND SKYLINE, BALTIMORE, MD.

119

*Purple-grey shadows and hot orange buildings enliven this linen card
of the Orleans Street Viaduct when it opened, and before traffic, in
1937. Harried motorists soon discovered it as an easier route for getting
from downtown to East Baltimore.*

War Memorial Plaza

War Memorial, Baltimore, Md.

120

A strange olive yellow dominates this linen of the War Memorial Building and its plaza in the early 1930s, with the Shot Tower perfectly positioned in the background. With its two horse statues in front, the building offers a perfect example of the "Government Deco" style.

DINE AND DANCE ON THE SPANISH VILLA

SOUTHERN HOTEL — BALTIMORE, MD.

*J*ust Passing Through

By the age of postcards, many landmark hostelries—like the Indian Queen, where Francis Scott Key completed his famous poem, or Barnum's, where Charles Dickens stayed—had disappeared. Of those pictured (figs. 121–33), only four still stand.

Eutaw House opened in 1835 at Eutaw and West Baltimore streets. During the Civil War, it briefly served as Gen. Lew Wallace's headquarters. Other guests included Henry Clay, Daniel Webster, Robert E. Lee, and Ulysses S. Grant. The Orioles and visiting teams dressed for games there. In 1912, a fire seriously damaged the building and the remainder was razed in 1916.

After 1905, stage personalities appearing at playhouses in the theatrical district around Howard and Franklin streets often stayed at the luxurious rococo-style Hotel Kernan, with its stained glass windows, Corinthian columns, and statuary. In the 1980s, the Marble Bar in what is now the Congress Hotel, was discovered by the rock-and-roll crowd.

Called the "Palace of the South" and known as a meeting place for Democratic politicians, the Rennert at Saratoga and Liberty streets reigned as one of Baltimore's most elegant hotels from 1885 until 1939. With prohibition's repeal in April 1933, its bar served as

The Spanish Villa (121), located on the rooftop of the Southern Hotel and exuberantly done up here, was a popular rendezvous in 1936, as this card makes clear. One of the earliest electric streetlights appears in the foreground of this 1912 view of Eutaw House (122) at Baltimore and Eutaw streets. The stylish Hotel Kernan (123), in the heart of Howard Street's theater district, even had an art gallery. Pictured in 1915, the hotel is now the Congress Hotel.

Eutaw House, Baltimore, Md.

122

16 Theatrical District showing the Maryland Auditorium and Academy Theatres, and The Kernan & Academy Hotel, Baltimore, Md

123

The Rennert Hotel (124), shown here in about 1912, earned fame for its food. H. L. Mencken recalled "there were two styles of crab soup on tap…and an oyster pot pie when I dined there daily." The hotel closed in 1939. Much plainer, the New Howard Hotel (125) presents a neat little building in this 1910 view. From its opening in 1903, the Belvedere (126) enjoyed a reputation as Baltimore's finest hotel. Encroaching structures have been removed in this card from about 1920.

124

Rennert Hotel,
Liberty and Saratoga Streets,
Baltimore, Md.

New Howard Hotel, Baltimore, Md.

125

126

BELVEDERE HOTEL, BALTIMORE, MD.

127

Lord Baltimore Hotel
Hanover and Baltimore Streets
Baltimore, Md.

128

THE EMERSON

BALTIMORE, MD. U.S.A.

129

The Southern Hotel
BALTIMORE   MARYLAND

The 1948 linen shows the Lord Baltimore Hotel
(127) much as it appears today. The Emerson
(128), built by Bromo-Seltzer millionaire Capt.
Isaac Emerson in 1911, is finely rendered in this
card from about 1924. For a 1943 linen of the
Southern Hotel (129), the artist selected a more
modern streamlined style of illustration and type.

a backdrop for the famous photograph of H. L. Mencken downing his first legal beer since 1920.

In the 1930s, the plain little New Howard on West Baltimore Street offered a luncheon special for fifty cents and a full-course dinner for only a dollar.

The Belvedere, Baltimore's best known grand hotel, rose in the Beaux Arts style of 1903 at Charles and Chase streets. Celebrities like Enrico Caruso, Mark Twain, and Marion Davies stayed there. The original Owl Bar continues, but the financially troubled hotel offers condominiums instead of guest rooms.

Built on the site of the Hotel Caswell on West Baltimore Street, the Lord Baltimore has greeted Maryland conventioneers and partygoers since 1928. The hotel's exterior, with its two carved-relief roundels of Lord Baltimore and an Indian chief at street level, looks much as it always has, except for the newer marble facing on the first floor.

On a warm day in about 1909 while dining at the Belvedere, Capt. Isaac Emerson removed his jacket. A waiter informed him that he could not. Reportedly the millionaire walked out, swearing that he would build his own hotel where he could do as he pleased. In 1911, he opened the Emerson at Baltimore and Calvert streets, and later added his own private penthouse suite. After

A wildly colorful art deco border clashes with the staid Hotel Altamont (130) in this 1932 linen. The Biltmore (131), a rather plain hotel on the outside, had a lobby that mixed old and new, as the coolly colored linen from 1949 shows.

130

131

Hotel Mayfair
Baltimore, Md.

ST. JAMES
HOTEL
Charles and Centre
Streets
Adjoining Beautiful
Mount Vernon Place
Baltimore 1,
Maryland

133

the Rennert closed, the Emerson served as Democratic headquarters and a home for visiting major league baseball teams through the early 1960s. On at least one occasion, visitors told of frogs jumping from the hotel's rooftop garden ponds into the décolletage of women on the street below. The fun ended with a huge auction in 1971.

Built on the site of the historic Fountain Inn, the Southern Hotel opened in 1918 during World War I, and the military uniforms of the Schuster Sisters' String Quintet in the Grill Room drew enthusiastic crowds. Guest rooms featured the new pointed electric light bulbs and shiny cuspidors. In the 1940s, live dance music from the hotel's "Spanish Villa" filled a nightly radio show. The hotel closed in 1964.

The aristocratic St. James Hotel stood at Charles and Centre streets for almost a century. Noted for its lobby chandelier, which took first prize at the 1893 Chicago World's Fair, it traditionally entertained a theatrical clientele. In 1963, a mysterious fire caused heavy damage and, four years later, crews demolished the once-proud hotel. (Sometime later, the young son of an actress in the *Sound of Music* confessed to setting this fire and similar ones in other cities on the show's schedule.)

Cars parked outside the Hotel Mayfair (132) help fix the date of this card at around 1948. The Blue Room, with its own entrance on the corner, was one of many bars in the 1300 block of North Charles Street at the time. The St. James (133), photographed in the mid-fifties, stood across from the Walters Art Gallery on Centre Street. Its French Gothic feel lent a touch of class to the neighborhood; the hotel was demolished in 1967.

Belgian Village
11 MILES NORTH OF BALTIMORE, MD. - U.S. ROUTE 40

134

CLAYTON'S TOURIST INN, ON U.S. ROUTE No. 1
IS 2 MILES SOUTH OF ELK RIDGE, MD.
10 MILES FROM MONTGOMERY-WARDS BALTIMORE
10 MILES FROM NEW YORK CITY   108 MILES FROM PHILADELPHIA
26 MILES FROM WASHINGTON   136 MILES FROM RICHMOND

135

136

T. V. Motel
AAA   Located on Pulaski Highway
U.S. Route 40
Midway between Aberdeen & Baltimore, Maryland

For a collector of motel postcards, this one of Belgian Village (134) from the early 1950s is a delight. The motel anticipates Disneyland in its unrestrained cuteness. By contrast, Clayton's Tourist Inn (135), "10 miles from Montgomery-Wards," displays a no-nonsense appearance in this view from about 1930. The obviously well kept T. V. Motel (136) reflects in its name another theme from the early 1950s.

137

TRAILER VILLAGE
8645 Pulaski Hwy. (U.S. 40)
Baltimore, Md.

138

City Chevrolet Co.
USED CAR MART
2507 North Howard Street
Baltimore 18, Maryland

$\mathcal{H}$itting the Road

The relative peace and prosperity of the 1950s meant that more and more people could afford to own cars and spend time driving them. Outside the city limits, they liked to speed up, turn on the radio, roll down the windows (before the days of air conditioning), and enjoy the sights. A Baltimore teenager in that decade might head for Beaver Dam, Gwynn Oak Park, the Varsity Inn, Ameche's, the Double T Diner, or Bel-Loc Diner. Before the interstate highway system sped things up, a longer journey to the ocean or into the mountains of any of half a dozen nearby states would give a driver a look at the best show in America—stuff by the side of the road.

Diners, ice cream stands, small-town coffee shops, flea markets, front-yard displays of hooked rugs and chenille bedspreads for sale, "tourist cabins" with "steam heat," or the ultimate luxury of a motel with a swimming pool were part of the fun of an automobile trip. Today, postcards of these pieces of roadside America from another era are highly valued by collectors.

Just down the highway, motorists found Trailer Village (137) with its neat striped awning and matching turquoise chairs. A pink convertible epitomized fifties style, and anyone in the market for a car found just the thing at City Chevrolet (138) in 1953.

The Flavor of the City

In the early years of this century, Baltimoreans particularly enjoyed dining on Chesapeake oysters, terrapin, and duck. Crabs were fried—the practice of steaming them in spicy seasonings did not gain popularity until the Depression years. A young H. L. Mencken remembered a friend eating thirty such fried hard crabs in one sitting, noting that "he not only ate them, but sucked the shells." Fresh saltwater oysters of several varieties delighted hungry visitors to raw bars like Dunlop's on Howard Street, where customers mixed their own cocktail sauce. In other establishments, customers soon discovered that shucking their own oysters took practice, as did learning to eat them right from the halfshell in all their juicy splendor.

Beer, of course, proved the natural beverage to accompany such feasts. Thanks to the city's large German population, no shortage of the drink hampered the eating habits of local consumers. In the same years, the German influence introduced the serving of coleslaw with seafood, while public schoolchildren found that other cabbage dish, sauerkraut, placed alongside their

In the kitchen of Duffy's Tavern (139) on Frederick Avenue in about 1940, cooks enthusiastically prepare the undisputed champion of Baltimore cuisine, hot steamed crabs (and plenty of them). The revamped establishment stands on the same spot today. At Childs' (140), things are noticeably more sedate in this card from 1908. A lunchroom filled daily with shoppers and office workers, it welcomed customers at Charles and Fayette streets twenty-four hours a day. Three small views of the Oyster Bay Restaurant (141) about 1940 reveal an art moderne decor inside and sleek front outside. It was in this restaurant on Christmas Eve 1949 that the original coach of the Colts, Cecil Isbell, first met his replacement, Walter Driskill.

143

NEW HOME ON OLD SITE—304 E. BALTIMORE ST., BALTIMORE, MD.

ARCHITECT—HENRY SMITH & SONS CO., BUILDERS

HORN & HORN, LUNCH ROO

Excellent Fare

MILLER BROS.

MILLER BROS. THE PLACE TO EAT

THE PLACE TO EAT

NATIONALLY FAMOUS
119 W. Fayette St.   Baltimore 1, Md.

142

CHUNGKING
SUPPER CLUB
110 N. Liberty St.
BALTIMORE 1, MD.
Located in the
Heart of Baltimore
America's
Most Beautiful
Theatre Restaurant
Cocktail Dancing
3 Floor Shows
Nightly

144

The Horn & Horn (143), another favorite
downtown eatery, welcomed well-dressed
Edwardian ladies and gentlemen in this
card promoting its opening in 1908
(the original building on the same site
fell victim to the famous 1904 fire).

Miller Brothers (142), one of the city's most
famous restaurants, occupied a building
that survived the Great Fire of 1904.
With flames licking around the corner
on Baltimore Street, firemen had already
drilled holes in the walls for dynamite
sticks to blast the building, but the wind
shifted and the structure was saved.
Besides its excellent food and a menu fea-
turing shark, whale, and other delicacies,
the place also boasted large aquariums
and caged canaries. The entrance appears
painted invitingly in this 1950s card.

GROTTO

COCKTAIL LOUNGE

4536 HARFORD ROAD • BALTIMORE, MARYLAND

145

Chinese Shrine

Jimmy Wu's
NEW CHINA INN
Baltimore, Md.

新中國酒家

146

Thanksgiving turkey and dressing, a tradition enjoyed today in many homes and restaurants.

In the search for interesting early cards, none appeared that depicted Baltimore's most famous restaurants, such as Haussner's, Marconi's, Martick's, Schellhase's, the best of Little Italy, or the Greek restaurants of Highlandtown. But local residents and visitors can hardly forget these places, and Baltimore restaurants continue to please palates in the city's finest tradition.

"America's Most Beautiful Theatre Restaurant," the ChungKing Supper Club (144) obviously offered more than dinner. Only one of many downtown watering holes for servicemen during World War II, it appears decorated for action (1944). Wonderfully streamlined and up-to-date in 1943, Munder's Lauraville House (145) made the most of its small triangular space on Harford Road. The display of food adds interest, but not as much as the striking decor of the cocktail lounge. A golden Chinese Shrine, a bartender named One Long Pour, as well as a case full of curiosities that included hundred-year-old eggs, made dining at Jimmy Wu's (146) fun. A popular spot before Oriole night games and after Sunday Colt games, the restaurant operated at its North Charles Street location for many years before it closed in 1983. This unusually colored linen is probably from the mid-fifties.

Watering Holes

Taverns, inns, and "watering holes" have long held an important place in the lives of Baltimoreans. Reportedly, the second house built on the town site of Baltimore was used as an inn for "Entertainment of Man and Beast." The Fountain Inn at Light and Redwood streets was known not only for its "frolicky assemblies" but as a place to conduct serious business. Before Congress declared war in 1812, Baltimore citizens met there to frame resolutions protesting British outrages on the high seas and calling for free trade and sailors' rights.

Goodwin's on South Calvert Street offered a back door where a banker could enter "to sell a railroad or dicker for a gold mine." Ex-Orioles Wilbert Robinson and John McGraw started the Diamond on Howard Street, "a great rallying place for the sports."

When the 1904 fire threatened Charlie's Place on Fayette Street, the innkeeper told his patrons to help themselves to food and drink. They did and then the wind changed. He was out a bundle of money but expressed no regrets.

During World War II, taverns provided a final evening of fun for soldiers who were "shipping out" for duty overseas.

The shiny undulating bar was the main attraction at the Sportsman (147), which in 1945 proudly displayed the "world's finest" collection of boxing photos. Everything in this bright, mid-fifties linen of the Club Charles (148) reminds us of an era when couples enjoyed a "night on the town," a romantic dinner followed by dancing to live music under a ceiling out of the Arabian Nights. In 1945, soldiers, sailors, and marines crowded into Benjamin's Bar and Lounge (149). With a red, white, and blue V for Victory, this multiple-view card gives us a marvelously detailed image of wartime Baltimore nightlife.

147

148

ONE SQUARE SOUTH OF UNION STATION

ONE SQUARE EAST OF MT. ROYAL STATION

SB-H717

CLUB CHARLES
CHARLES ST.
AT PRESTON,
BALTIMORE, MD.

COCKTAILS BAR

Benjamin's BAR & LOUNGE

KEEP SMILING

Your Friend Benny

A NIGHT at BENJAMIN'S BAR and LOUNGE

BENJAMIN'S BAR and COCKTAIL LOUNGE — 312 W. FAYETTE ST. — BALTIMORE 1, MD.

The Fifth Regiment Armory

The Fifth Maryland Regiment, known as the "Dandy Fifth," originated in the famous Maryland Line of the Continental army. One of the oldest military units in the country, it has its home in this massive stone structure built in 1901 at Howard and Preston streets. The first armory to house the Maryland National Guard, the building served as the temporary address of several businesses in need of office space after the great fire in 1904.

The Democratic National Convention nominated Woodrow Wilson here in 1912, and it was the site of a Franklin D. Roosevelt speech a few weeks before his 1932 election. A fire a year later damaged most of the building and destroyed the barrel roof. Rebuilding in 1934 saved most of the original stone walls but flattened the roof.

Bird's Eye View of Mount Royal Ave. Looking towards B. & O. Station

151

150

FIFTH REGIMENT ARMORY, WEST HOFFMAN STREET, BALTIMORE, MD

Proudly strolling by the Fifth Regiment Armory (150) just after World War I, these soldiers and civilians have been completely invented by the artist, who also added the flag. Here in 1912, on the forty-sixth ballot, Woodrow Wilson won the presidential nomination at the Democratic National Convention. Still the home of the 29th Division, the armory today has a flat roof. The original barrel roof, seen here, collapsed in a fire in 1933.

Mount Royal Avenue

Mount Royal Avenue (151) in 1922 had wide sidewalks and congested parking, as this adventurously colored but crudely printed card demonstrates. The left side of the street has changed greatly, but the B&O station's clock tower in the center, the large red brick Lyric Opera House, and the Garage building (where all the cars are parked) still stand. With several car dealerships, stores, lunch counters, and a bowling alley under its wide roof, the Garage (152) attracted a variety of patrons. Now the University of Baltimore's Academic Center, the building looks much as it does in this card, which bears a 1911 postmark.

The Garage,
Mt. Royal Avenue and Charles Street,
Baltimore, Md.

An unusually wide, curving thoroughfare that first took horse-drawn buggies and then automobiles from downtown out to the greenery of Druid Hill Park, Mount Royal Avenue today styles itself as the "cultural corridor" of Baltimore. Within a three or four block radius stand the Maryland Institute College of Art, the Lyric Opera House, the Meyerhoff Symphony Hall, and the University of Baltimore. Each July the city's celebration of the creative spirit, Artscape, draws thousands of visitors to the avenue.

The blocks closest to Druid Hill feature some of the finest examples of stone-and-brick townhouses in the city, along with the Gothic revival Corpus Christi Catholic Church. At the center of the curve stands the striking grey stone clock tower of old Mount Royal Station, a symbol of the area. The entire station building now serves as part of the Maryland Institute, which has replaced the B&O passenger waiting room—famous for its homey rocking chairs and golden oak trim—with its own studios, library, auditorium, and gallery.

The Garage opened in 1906 as an auto showroom. Soon after, it also had a roller-skating rink, gymnasium, and at least one restaurant. After standing empty for years, today it is the Academic Center of the University of Baltimore. The expert renovation and restoration of the building which retained most of its original character earned a citation from Baltimore Heritage in 1971 as the most important example of adaptive reuse.

The Water

In a city built around a harbor, it comes as no surprise that Baltimoreans have always had a close connection with the water. Some people view it as the perfect place to spend lazy summer days swimming, sailing, or sportfishing with friends on creeks, rivers, lakes, or the bay. Many rugged individuals, seemingly oblivious to the weather, choose to earn their livelihood by harvesting crabs, oysters, and fish to be sold at local markets or shipped to other parts of the country. Others work at the port loading locally manufactured goods on distant-sailing merchant ships or at the dry docks repairing vessels that ply the seas. There are also those who work high above the water, maintaining the safety and appearance of the numerous bridges that span the rivers and the bay.

In the middle part of this century, Baltimore's Inner Harbor (once described by Mencken as "so rotten, it smelled like a billion polecats") languished amid rotting piers and derelict warehouses. Many residents thought nothing could be done to make it a place that people would actually choose to visit. Others in business and politics had a different view and spearheaded the movement to resurrect the waterside. In 1976, as part of the nation's bicentennial celebration, tall ships from distant ports dropped anchor here, heralding the beginning of the renaissance. When Harborplace opened in 1980, pleasure boats began bringing countless visitors to enjoy the restaurants, shops, and museums that now ring the harbor in a still-widening circle.

Fair View on the Patapsco, Baltimore, Md.

153

5

Maryland Yacht Club, Baltimore, Maryland

154

74

CHESAPEAKE BAY BRIDGE on U.S. ROUTE 50,
Linking Western and Eastern Shores of Maryland

155

Hanover Street Bridge, Baltimore, Md.

156

Fair View Beach on the Patapsco (153), with its picnic ground, carousel, and swimming area, was a popular turn-of-the-century steamer destination from Baltimore. Probably on a Sunday outing in 1906, these young men pose on the deck of their small boat under a sky only an artist could imagine; meanwhile, a lady sits just as comfortably in the shade.

In a linen from about 1950, a blazing sunset marks the end of a good day's boating and sailing for members of the Maryland Yacht Club (154), shown at its original location in Broening Park. The oldest such club on the bay, it was formed in 1908 and has since moved to Rock Creek in Pasadena, near old Fair View Beach.

In a view never enjoyed by motorists, the brand new Chesapeake Bay Bridge (155) looms high above the viewer in 1952. Its nearly four-and-a-half-mile span across the water meant that travelers no longer had to take the northern drive around the bay or the ferries to Love Point and other Eastern Shore landings. Fishermen and crabbers soon discovered successful harvests directly under the bridge.

The Hanover Street Bridge (156) stretches for almost a mile over the unbelievably blue water of the Patapsco in this linen from the 1940s. Linking downtown with Brooklyn and Curtis Bay, the bridge opened for traffic in 1916, replacing the old, wooden Long Bridge, which ran from the foot of Light Street.

The Walters Art Gallery

157

Walters Art Gallery, Charles and Centre Streets, Baltimore, Md.   3B-H739

In front of the Walters Art Gallery in 1943—in the days of gas rationing—
a lone automobile in an otherwise empty street heads in what today
is the wrong direction on Charles Street. Henry Walters opened this
Renaissance revival structure to the public in 1909. It houses the impres-
sive collection that he built over more than forty years and that he left
to the city in 1931.

The Baltimore Museum of Art

Museum of Art, Baltimore, Maryland   18

In about 1950, cool purple shadows and bright sunny walls color what is actually the grey-stone exterior of the Baltimore Museum of Art. Opened in 1929 and added to extensively since then, it is Maryland's largest art museum, housing over 100,000 objects, and offers visitors delights ranging from ancient mosaics to contemporary art.

The Women's Industrial Exchange

WOMAN'S INDUSTRIAL EXCHANGE   BALTIMORE, MD.

159

At the busy corner of Charles and East Pleasant streets, the Women's Industrial Exchange showcases a bright window full of handmade items. This extraordinarily clear and finely hand colored card dates from 1929 or 1930, when the Exchange neared its fiftieth year.

Baltimore Belles

Pretty girls,
pretty girls
everywhere,
But the
BALTIMORE
BELLES
are claimed
most fair.

Baltimore, Court House.

160

That these "belles" are actually from Baltimore is unlikely since this card is one of the "Our Belles" series that simply substituted a new city name and image for dozens of locations. Published by the famous Raphael Tuck & Sons of London, it has two clear 1908 postmarks.

161

With exuberant hand lettering and saturated colors typical of the period, this linen with predictable images celebrates the city in 1941.

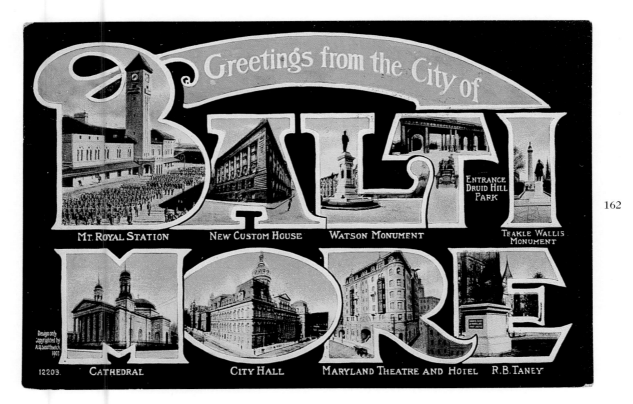

162

Well-known landmarks and graceful hand lettering fill this adventurously designed card. Copyrighted in 1907, it bears a 1909 postmark.

163

PIMLICO RACE TRACK, NEAR BALTIMORE, MD.

164

Tomb of Edgar Allan Poe, Baltimore, Md.

Baltimoreans have always loved a good horse race, and Pimlico Racetrack (163) has obliged them since 1870. The home of the Preakness, the second jewel in the Triple Crown, Pimlico in about 1925 stands empty. The lovely wooden clubhouse burned to the ground in 1966.

A carved likeness of the great American writer and inventor of horror stories Edgar Allan Poe stares out from his grave marker (164) in this 1940s linen card. Poe, who lived for a time in Baltimore, was the grandson of David Poe, the city's deputy commissary general during the Revolution. The writer died in Baltimore in 1849 and lies buried in the cemetery of Westminster Church at Fayette and Greene streets.

Collecting Baltimore Postcards

My modest collection of postcards currently stands at around 3,000, with almost 500 of Baltimore alone, but I know collectors who have thousands of Baltimore cards. I have gathered and saved cards mailed to me or my family since childhood and brought cards home from vacations since high school. When the Marine Corps shipped me to six countries in three years and I found myself living out of a seabag, postcards of every port of call were all I had room for in the way of souvenirs. I still have these after thirty years, and looking at them now brings me immense pleasure. But my serious collecting did not begin until I started attending paper collectible shows with their labels, posters, and ephemera that were a natural extension of my interest in graphic design, and I noticed boxes and albums of old postcards. I spent some time fingering through them, and immediately saw what caring craftsmen did with ink on paper long ago. I liked the wildly exaggerated linens as well as the softer colorings and documentary quality of earlier cards. In short, I was hooked.

At first, like most novice collectors, I bought junk—torn, smudged, or common cards for a dollar or two—but I quickly developed an eye for judging a card and, more important, I determined the categories I wanted to acquire. A new collector, full of adrenaline for the hunt at a show where he or she will easily spend three or four hours (after that my eyes glaze over and all the cards start to look alike), can waste a lot of that time being distracted by dealer displays. Expensive hold-to-lights, Santa Claus, and Halloween cards still stop me in my tracks.

Once you know what interests you—Baltimore, or any town in Maryland or in any other state—you can search a dealer's categories for treasures not seen in your particular file. For example, motels on Route 40 might be under "motels," while diners on Pulaski Highway might have their own category, and Friendship Airport might be under "aircraft" or "aviation." Of course, you will often find three or four versions of the same view; companies reissued certain popular cards every few years. It was an easy task, since the images began as black-and-white photos that were painted over, and the style could change from delicate to crude to downright gaudy, with gold ink or glitter added. Choosing which view of the Shot Tower you want is part of the fun, and arranging your album pages to show off six or seven cards of the same subject is very satisfying. Advertising is another means for Baltimore collectors to find cards from businesses that ceased to exist years ago, like O'Neill's, Monumental Motor Tours, or the Peabody Book Shop and Beer Stube.

Most dealers are happy to spend time educating a new collector on the finer points of a chosen category, so getting to know a dealer by going to a show or visiting a shop is time well spent. Look in the yellow pages under "Postcards." Good places to pick up old cards include book shows, antiquarian book dealers, estate auctions, and even flea markets. Several price guides to postcards exist in paperback; there are also one or two books on postcard history. You do not have to be wealthy to enjoy postcard collecting as a hobby, and you will find an amazing assortment of subjects to tempt you. Baltimore is only one of nine or ten categories I collect, but that's another story, and perhaps another book.

About the Postcards

No.	Title	Publisher	Code	Year
80	Observatory, Patterson Park	Ottenheimer	PM	1911
81	Clifton Park Swimming Pool	Chessler, #8789		c1930
82	Johns Hopkins Mansion, Clifton Park	Ottenheimer, #8494	PM	1910
83	Electric Park at Night	Unknown, #180-24	PM	1912
84	Dancing Pavilion, Gwynn Oak Park	Smith, #174	HD	1910
85	Bay Shore Park	Rinn, #619	PM	1916
86	Bird's Eye View of the Amusement Section, Carlin's Park	Cann, #44451		c1940
87	The Baltimore Stadium, 33rd Street Boulevard	Ottenheimer		c1932
88	Baltimore Stadium	Calvert News Co., #71008	PM	1944
89	Memorial Stadium	D. E. Traub, Baltimore, #P14965		1954
90	"Tis the star spangled banner"	International Art Pub. Co, NY		c1909
91	Fort McHenry	Rinn, #6	PM	1908
92	The Human Flag, Fort McHenry	Ottenheimer	PM	1922
93	Entrance to Fort McHenry	Albertype	HC	c1909
94	Home of the "Star-Spangled Banner"	Tichnor, #70982	PM	1947
95	White Steps in Baltimore	Calvert News Co.		c1935
96	Greyhound Bus Terminal	Ottenheimer, CT #3B-H71	PM 1943	1943
97	Camden Station	Chessler & Oberender, #3409		c1918
98	Mount Royal Station	Ottenheimer, #7681	PM	1908
99	The William Crooks Train	B&O Railroad Co.		1927
100	B&O Railroad, Fair of the Iron Horse	B&O Railroad Co.	RP	1927
101	New Union Station by Night	Ottenheimer	PM	1922
102	Yankee Clipper	Calvert, T #70995		c1940
103	Seaplanes at Baltimore's Transatlantic Air Base	Cann, #47335	PM	1941
104	Glenn L. Martin Aircraft Plant	Ottenheimer, CT #9A-H1601	PM 1942	1939
105	Main Lobby, Friendship Airport	Ottenheimer, CT #4C-H90		1954
106	Observation Ramp, Friendship Airport	Ottenheimer, CT #4C-H89		1954
107	Public School No. 55, Hampden	Rinn, #705	PM	1910
108	Bryn Mawr School	Albertype	HC	c1910
109	Public School No. 98	Rinn, #664	PM	1911
110	City College	Metro Craft, #47323		c1932
111	New Eastern High School	Ottenheimer, CT #8A-H1655		1938
112	Polytechnic Institute	Ottenheimer, R 59474		c1925
113	Western High School	Ottenheimer, R 34852		1920
114	Mechanical Hall, Johns Hopkins University	Ottenheimer, R 63622		c1925
115	State Normal School	Chessler, #69		c1925
116	Goucher College	Cann, #85		c1920
117	Maryland Institute	Ottenheimer, #8512		1909
118	Peabody Institute	Tichnor, #70985		c1939
119	New Viaduct and Skyline	Levin, #40594	PM	1938
120	War Memorial	Tichnor, #70979		c1940
121	Southern Hotel's Spanish Villa	CT #6A-H485		1936
122	Eutaw House	Unknown, #12219	HD	1910
123	Theatrical District	Chessler, #3415	PM	1915
124	Rennert Hotel	Ottenheimer, #A-14562		c1912
125	New Howard Hotel	Ottenheimer, #214		c1910
126	Belvedere Hotel	Ottenheimer, #R-70245		c1920
127	Lord Baltimore Hotel	Ottenheimer, CT #8B-H1141		1948
128	The Emerson	Unknown		c1924
129	The Southern Hotel	Teich, #3B H456		1943
130	Hotel Altamont	Teich, #2A-110		1932
131	The Biltmore Hotel	CT #9B-H527		1949
132	Hotel Mayfair	Color Picture, Boston, #K3873		c1948
133	St. James Hotel	Chas. D. Holland, Baltimore, #40624		c1955
134	Belgian Village	Unknown, #10,379		c1950
135	Clayton's Tourist Inn, on U.S. Route 1	Hartman Card Co., Portland, ME, #134390		c1930
136	T.V. Motel	Mellinger Studios, Lancaster, PA		1954
137	Trailer Village	R. C. Shaul, Chicago, #27666N		c1950
138	City Chevrolet	Unknown	PM	1953
139	Duffy's Tavern	Rollman & Schloss, Baltimore #11,518F		c1940
140	A Childs' Place	The Platinachrome Co., NY		c1908
141	Oyster Bay Restaurant	Unknown, #12,023F		c1940
142	Miller Brothers	Embetone, Frederick, MD	Foldout	c1950
143	Horn & Horn, Lunch Rooms	Unknown		c1908
144	ChungKing Supper Club	Teich, #4B-H1510		1944
145	Munder's Lauraville House	Teich, #3B-H1448		1943
146	Jimmy Wu's New China Inn	E. J. Hartung, Baltimore, #14,078		c1955
147	Sportsman Bar	Teich, #5B-H717		1945
148	Club Charles	Tichnor, #76444		1955
149	Benjamin's Bar and Cocktail Lounge	Teich, #5B-H28		1945
150	Fifth Regiment Armory	Ottenheimer, #70926		c1920
151	Bird's Eye View of Mount Royal Avenue	Cann, #19897		c1922
152	The Garage	Smith, #A-17651	PM	1911
153	Fair View on the Patapsco	Smith	UB	1906
154	Maryland Yacht Club	Cann Color Picture #K 3076		c1950
155	Chesapeake Bay Bridge, on U.S. Route 50	Cann		1952
156	Hanover Street Bridge	Calvert News Co., T #73454		c1945
157	Walters Art Gallery	Ottenheimer, CT #3B-H739	PM 1948	1943
158	Museum of Art	Cann Color Picture, #K 3089		c1950
159	Wom[e]n's Industrial Exchange	Hugh Gwynn, Baltimore	HC	1930
160	Baltimore Belles	Raphael Tuck & Sons, London, #2740	PM	1908
161	Greetings from Baltimore	Ottenheimer, CT #1B-H1591		1941
162	Greetings from the City of Baltimore	A. O. Southwick, #12203	PM	1909
163	Pimlico Racetrack	Ottenheimer, CT #7199		c1925
164	Tomb of Edgar Allan Poe	Calvert News Co., T #70990		c1940

Key: c - circa; CT - Curt Teich; T - Tichnor; HC - hand colored; HD - hand dated; PM - postmarked; UB - undivided back; RP - real photo.

About the Author

Bert Smith is a graphic designer who has worked in print and television in Baltimore and elsewhere for more than twenty-five years. He teaches in the nationally recognized graduate program in publications design at the University of Baltimore, from which he received his M.A. in 1985. After graduating from City College and serving for three years in the Marine Corps, he earned a B.F.A. from the Maryland Institute College of Art and designed the first television newsgraphics for the Baltimore market at WJZ-TV from 1974 to 1976. Mr. Smith's illustrations, design, and typography have won awards from the New York Art Director's Club, *Print* Magazine, the American Institute of Graphic Arts, *Graphic Design: USA*, and the Printing Industries of America. Other books he has designed or art-directed include *Kitty Hawk and Beyond: The Wright Brothers and the Early Years of Aviation; West Baltimore Neighborhoods; and Deus Loci, The Lawrence Durrell Journal.* He lives with his wife, Anthea, also an award-winning artist, in the Hampden section of the city he writes about.